Oxford
New Enjoying Mathematics

CLASS **5**

Aashalata Badami

Series Editor
Jose Paul

OXFORD
UNIVERSITY PRESS

OXFORD
UNIVERSITY PRESS

Oxford University Press is a department of the University of Oxford
It furthers the University's objective of excellence in research, scholarship,
and education by publishing worldwide. Oxford is a registered trademark of
Oxford University Press in the UK and in certain other countries

Published in India by
Oxford University Press
YMCA Library Building, 1 Jai Singh Road, New Delhi 110001, India

First published 2006
Second revised edition 2009
Fifth impression 2012

ISBN-13: 978-0-19-569453-6
ISBN-10: 0-19-569453-8

Typeset in Times New Roman
by Star Compugraphics, Delhi 110096
Printed in India by Repro India Ltd., Navi Mumbai

Illustrations by Pankajakshan K, Amit John
Santosh Gupta, Pradeep Nayak, and Nilabho Dhar Chowdhury

Preface

Mathematics is a dynamic subject—it is constantly changing and can never be static. It challenges us to new horizons and forces us to look at new goals. For an enjoyable experience of mathematics, we must necessarily be able to relate the subject to the environment and focus on the development of thinking and reasoning skills. Keeping this in mind, this revised edition of *Enjoying Mathematics,* while drawing strength from the previous edition, enriches itself on its new features.

New Enjoying Mathematics is a carefully graded series of nine books that conforms to the vision of the National Curriculum Framework (2005) and meets the requirements of the new 2005 NCERT Syllabus for mathematics. This series furthers the NCERT's objective of shifting away from rote learning by linking school knowledge with a child's everyday experience.

The revised edition continues to follow the same philosophy and belief as of the original, where mathematics is treated as more than just formulae and calculation techniques. It aims at building real-life skills in children who are taught to think, deduce and reason, rather than just deal with mechanical procedures. This is done keeping the child's level of understanding and interests in mind. It sets out to first build concepts thoroughly before moving onto the essential drill and practice. Wherever required, appropriate illustrations have been inserted to help in visualization of abstract mathematical concepts.

Key Features

- *Looking Back* for refreshing the concepts learnt earlier
- *Chapter Check-up* at the end of each chapter for easy recapitulation
- *Worksheets* to integrate mathematics with other subjects of the curriculum
- *Challenge* questions to build thinking skills beyond the level of classroom learning
- *Enrichment Time* and *Activity Bag* to explore the subject and think creatively
- *Mental Maths* questions to help the students to do calculations quickly
- *Maths Lab Activities* to help build concepts through different activities

Additional Features of the new edition

- All pages from Introductory book to Book 5 in full colour.
- **Increased** number of questions in the exercises, including word problems
- **Project** in every chapter to help students connect the topics with everyday life
- **Keeping in touch** to enable children to revisit the concepts previously learnt
- **Test your skills**—a cumulative revision page after every three chapters with the objective of helping children remember previously learnt concepts
- **New topics in NCERT** syllabus have been included

My sincerest thanks to the dedicated editing, design and production teams at Oxford University Press for their motivated and inspired inputs. I would also like to thank the dynamic sales and marketing team through whose untiring efforts this book has reached thousands of students and teachers across the country. My special thanks also to several teachers who took time out of busy schedules to give us invaluable feedback and suggestions, many of which have been incorporated.

A project can achieve what it sets out to do only with blessings from above, and I am grateful for that. And finally, I thank my family for their support, their patience and for always being there for me.

Aashalata Badami

CONTENTS

Place Value

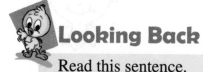

Looking Back

Read this sentence.
India has 65,590 km of National Highways and 1,31,899 km of State Highways.

L	TTh	Th	H	T	O
1	3	1	8	9	9

— 9
— 90
— 800
— 1,000
— 30,000
—1,00,000

65,590

↓

These digits tell us how many thousands.

1,31,899

↓

This digit tells us how many lakhs.

In words: One lakh thirty-one thousand eight hundred ninety-nine

Expanded notation: 1,00,000 + 30,000 + 1000 + 800 + 90 + 9

1. **Use the digits 5, 6, 3, 8, 9, 1 to:**
   (a) build the greatest number possible.
   (b) build the smallest number possible.
   (c) give the expanded notation and number name for both.

2. **Fill in the blanks.**
   (a) 75 rounded to the nearest 10 is _____
   (b) 174 rounded to the nearest 10 is _____
   (c) 176 rounded to the nearest 100 is _____

Lakhs and Crores

I am Remo. I live in Goa. Goa has a population of 13,47,668. This number is too big for me to read!

I am Surjeet. I live in Delhi. My city has 1,38,50,507 people. I need help to read this big number!

Let us help Remo and Surjeet read these large numbers.

Let us begin with Remo's number.

13,47,668 is a 7-digit number.

Do you remember the largest 6-digit number?

If you add 1 to it you get the smallest 7-digit number.

$$
\begin{array}{r}
9,99,999 \\
+\ 1 \\
\hline
10,00,000
\end{array}
$$

10,00,000 is ten lakh.

↳ These digits tell you how many lakhs.

13,47,668

These digits tell you how many lakhs ← | → These digits tell you how many thousands

Now I can read it!
Thirteen lakh forty-seven thousand six hundred sixty-eight.

Try This

Read out these numbers aloud.

(a) 23,18,964   (b) 11,00,893   (c) 70,28,310   (d) 41,08,239

Take the number 27,68,435.

Lakhs		Thousands		Ones		
TL	L	TTh	Th	H	T	O
2	7	6	8	4	3	5

← Period

← Place

TL stands for ten lakh.

In words: Twenty-seven lakh sixty-eight thousand four hundred thirty-five
In figures: 27,68,435

Expanded notation:
20,00,000 + 7,00,000 + 60,000 + 8,000 + 400 + 30 + 5

27,00,000   68,000   435

27,68,000

27,68,435

Remember

- A 7-digit number begins at the **ten lakhs** place.
- The ten lakhs place is in the lakhs period.

8-Digit Numbers

Let's look at Surjeet's number now. 1,38,50,507 people live in Delhi.
1,38,50,507 is an 8-digit number.
The largest 7-digit number is
If you add 1 to it
It becomes one hundred lakh.

$$\begin{array}{r} 99,99,999 \\ +\ \ \ \ 1 \\ \hline 100,00,000 \end{array}$$

One hundred lakh is also called one crore.

1,00,00,000
→ This digit tells you how many crores

1 , 38 , 50 , 507

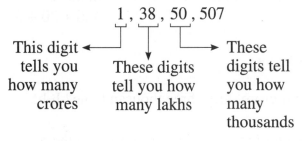

This digit tells you how many crores

These digits tell you how many lakhs

These digits tell you how many thousands

Try This

Read out these numbers aloud.

(a) 2,38,49,364   (b) 5,09,36,400
(c) 7,19,00,861   (d) 2,00,53,090

So there are one crore, thirty-eight lakh, fifty thousand, five hundred seven people living in my city.

Remember

- An 8-digit number begins with the one crores (C) place. 1 crore has 7 zeros.
- The one crores place is in the crores period.
- 10 ten lakhs (100 lakhs) = 1 crore
- We put a comma or leave space to separate the crores period from the lakhs period.

8-digit number means we move one place further to the left in the place-value chart.

Take the number 9,27,68,435.

It is easy to read a number with three commas. The first comma says crore, the second, says lakh, the third comma says thousand.

Crores	Lakhs		Thousands		Ones		
C	TL	L	T Th	Th	H	T	O
9	2	7	6	8	4	3	5

9   27   68   435

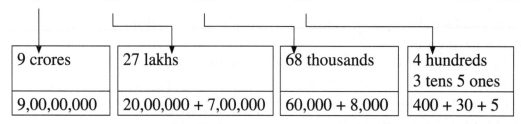

9 crores	27 lakhs	68 thousands	4 hundreds 3 tens 5 ones
9,00,00,000	20,00,000 + 7,00,000	60,000 + 8,000	400 + 30 + 5

In words: Nine crore twenty-seven lakh sixty-eight thousand four hundred thirty-five.
In figures: 9,27,68,435 (with commas) or 9 27 68 435 (with space)
Expanded notation: 9,00,00,000 + 20,00,000, + 7,00,000, + 60,000 + 8,000 +
400 + 30 + 5

Understanding Numbers Better

How do I write the number four crore, fifty-three thousand one? It has no lakhs!
Write the place-value chart and fill in the numbers according to the periods and places.

C	TL	L	T Th	Th	H	T	O
4			5	3			1

Then fill in all the vacant places with zeros.

C	TL	L	T Th	Th	H	T	O
4	0	0	5	3	0	0	1

Answer: 4,00,53,001

How do I find the number before and after a large number?

You can think of the number after as '+1' and the number before as '–1'

The number **after** 56,79,999 is 56,80,000.
The number **before** 6,78,800 is 6,78,799.

Let us compare numbers now.

My number is
5,67,890

My number is
11,98,087

5,67,890 < 11,98,087

The number with more digits is the bigger number.

Now I pick
76,87,858

I pick
76,89,663

- Start from the left and compare the digits until you find two digits that are different.

76,87,858 < 76,89,663

7 6 8 7 8 5 8
7 6 8 9 6 6 3

Same   Different
7 < 9

What comes next?

23,45,678	40,46,300
23,46,678	40,56,300
23,47,678	40,66,300
?	?

Answer: 23,48,678   *Answer:* 40,76,300

How many numbers have 4 digits?
Let us start by finding out how many numbers have 1, 2, and 3 digits. We may find a pattern!

(a) The smallest one-digit number is 1.
The greatest one-digit number is 9.
   9 − 1 = 8
   8 + 1 = 9
There are 9 one-digit numbers.

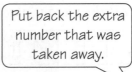
Put back the extra number that was taken away.

(b) Smallest 2-digit number is 10.
Greatest 2-digit number is 99.
   99 − 10 = 89
   89 + 1 = 90
There are 90 two-digit numbers.

(c) Smallest 3-digit number is 100.
Greatest 3-digit number is 999.
   999 − 100 = 899
   899 + 1 = 900
There are 900 three-digit numbers.

I can see the pattern!
1-digit numbers – 9
2-digit numbers – 90
3-digit numbers – 900

There must be 9000 4-digit numbers!

Try This

There are:

_____ 5-digit numbers
_____ 6-digit numbers
_____ 7-digit numbers
_____ 8-digit numbers

Exercise 1.1

1.

Clues across	Clues down
(1) The value of a digit is divided by this number as it moves to the right in the place value chart.	(1) Give the difference between the face value and the place value of the digit 2 in the number 5,27,87,890.
(6) How much is 10,000 more than 23,38,901?	(2) How much is 1,00,000 less than 64,45,121.
(4) The largest two digit number.	(3) Give the next number in the pattern. 38 33 659, 38 43 659, 38 53 659
(7) Rearrange the digits 3, 7, 5, 2, 5, 9, 0, 0, 6 to form the biggest number possible.	(4) How many six digit numbers are there in all?
(8) Give the next number in the pattern. 80,11,497 81,11,497 82,11,497	(5) Give the standard form of ninety-one lakh twenty thousand four hundred twelve.

2. **If you are 10 years old, you would have lived 52,56,000 minutes. Compare the numbers given below and match the age to the minutes lived. Do not calculate. Match by putting the numbers in ascending order.**

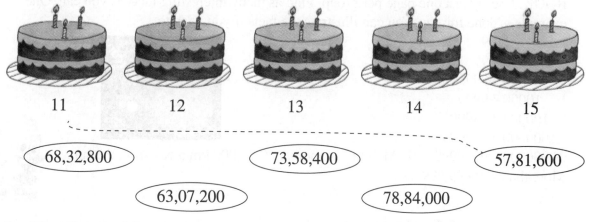

11   12   13   14   15

68,32,800   73,58,400   57,81,600

63,07,200   78,84,000

3. **Give the word form and the expanded notation for these numbers.**
   (a) 67,09,654   (b) 79,00,690   (c) 9,83,10,809   (d) 2,10,23,008   (e) 45,00,091

4. **Write in figures (with commas).**
   (a) Eight lakh thirty-nine thousand twenty-three
   (b) Twenty lakh nine hundred five
   (c) Thirty-five thousand eight hundred fifty-seven
   (d) Eighty-three lakh nine hundred
   (e) Four crore thirty-seven lakh nineteen thousand

5. **Give the place value of the coloured digit.**
   (a) 89,00,345   (b) 30,34,112   (c) 87,93,389   (d) 2,67,23,592   (e) 7,08,19,004

6. **Compare using <, >, or =.**
   (a) 5,87,90,456 ◯ 5,78,23,567   (b) 90,40,908 ◯ 9,04,908
   (c) 8,20,45,899 ◯ 8,20,54,899   (d) 1,40,10,178 ◯ 1,40,10,720

7. **Make the smallest possible 7-digit number by repeating the digits.**
   (a) 5, 8, 2, 9, 1   (b) 4, 7, 1, 9, 0

8. **Make the smallest and the greatest possible 8-digit number by repeating the digits.**
   (a) 3, 6, 1, 7, 8, 9, 2   (b) 4, 7, 1, 0, 3, 5

9. **Give the number before:**
   (a) 45,69,500   (b) 87,16,000
   (c) 5,10,000   (d) 20,00,000

10. **Give the number after:**
   (a) 9,29,499   (b) 79,98,999
   (c) 99,99,999   (d) 1,98,97,950

Project

Make a "FACT BOOK".
Research facts in encyclopedias or on the internet to fit in these groups of your FACT BOOK. Use at least one page per group. Find as many interesting facts as you can. One example is done for you. You can illustrate the facts if you wish to.

      1–99
     100–999
    1000–9999
   10000–99999
  100000–999999
1000000–9999999
10000000–99999999 ⟶ Mercury is about 5,79,37,000 km away from the sun.
More than–9,99,99,999

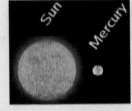

International System

2 3 4 1 9 6

In India we read this number as Two lakh thirty-four thousand one hundred ninety-six.
2,34,196

In my country this is Two hundred thirty-four thousand and one hundred ninety-six
234,196

Lakh	TTh	Th	H	T	O	Indian System
Hundred Thousand	TTh	Th	H	T	O	International System

Common

1 2 3 4 1 9 6

This is twelve lakh thirty-four thousand one hundred ninety-six (12,34,196) in the Indian system.

In the International system, this is one million two hundred thirty-four thousand one hundred ninety-six (1,234,196).

Ten Lakhs	Lakh	TTh	Th	H	T	O	Indian System
Million	Hundred Thousand	TTh	Th	H	T	O	International System

Remember

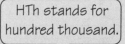

HTh stands for hundred thousand.

- 5-digit numbers are read the same way in both the systems.
- 6-digit numbers are read differently because what we call a **lakh** in the Indian system is called a **hundred thousand** in the International system.
- 7-digit numbers are called **million** in the International system.
- There is no comma after the hundred thousand in the International system.
- There is a comma after the million place.
- A 6-digit number has 1 comma and a 7-digit number has 2 commas.

I use this trick to remember the zeros in a million.

M	I	L	L	I	O	N
1	0	0	0	0	0	0

Read these figures.

(a) 439,168—Four hundred thirty-nine thousand one hundred sixty-eight

(b) 1,201,590—One million two hundred one thousand five hundred ninety

(c) 5,500,109—Five million five hundred thousand one hundred nine

Exercise 1.2

1. **Put the commas using the International system and rewrite these statements using the word form of the number.**
   (a) There are more than 400000 species of plants in the plant kingdom.
   (b) There are about 250000 flowering plants.
   (c) Mr Acharya's new house costs Rs 1703800.
   (d) Himachal Pradesh has a population of 6077900.

2. Find 6- and 7-digit numbers in the newspapers and rewrite them using the International system.

Rounding

The figure used in this newspaper headline is a rounded figure.

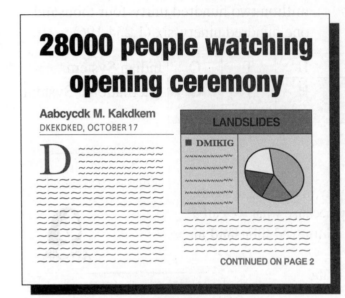

CONTINUED ON PAGE 2

Rules of Rounding

Revise the rules of rounding.

- When we round a number to the nearest 10, we use the **nearest multiple of 10.**
- When we round a number to the nearest 100, we use the **nearest multiple of 100.**
- When we round a number to the nearest 1,000, we use the **nearest multiple of 1,000.**

(a) Round 1,135 to the nearest 10.

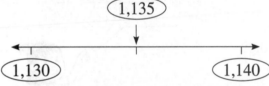

1,135 is between 1,130 and 1,140.
1,135 is exactly halfway between 1,130 and 1,140.
As per the rule, **1,135 has to be rounded up to 1,140.**

A number at the midway point is always rounded up.

(b) Round 7,750 to the nearest 100.
7,750 comes between 7,700 and 7,800.
7,750 is halfway between 7,700 and 7,800.
As per the rule, **7,750 is rounded up to 7,800.**

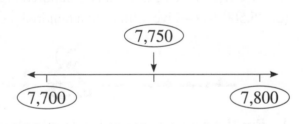

(c) Round 2,625 to the nearest 1,000.
You can also think of the number line as a series of hills and valleys.

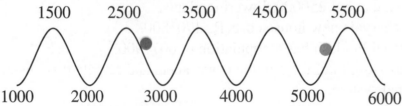

Imagine a ball at the number 2,625. It would roll down to the number 3,000.
2,625 rounded to the nearest 1,000 is 3,000.
A ball at 5,324 would roll back to 5,000.
5,324 rounded to the nearest 1,000 is 5,000.

(d) 27,454 people attended the opening
ceremony of the Asian Games.
How will you round the figure to the nearest 1,000?
Round 27,454 to the nearest 1,000.
27,454 is between 27,000 and 28,000.
27,454 is closer to 27,000.
Answer: 27,454 is rounded down to 27,000.

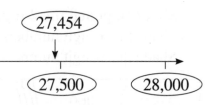

Use a Shortcut!

Round 17,678 to the nearest 1,000.
Step 1: Find the digit in the place that you are
rounding to ——→ 1**7**,678
Step 2: Look at the digit to its right ——→ 17,**6**78
Step 3: Since 6 is more than 5, add 1 to the digit in
the thousands place and **change** all the digits
after that to 0. ——→ 18,000
Answer: 17,678 rounded to the nearest 1,000 is 18,000.

In Step 3 if the digit is less than 5, then keep the rounding place as it is and change the digits that follow it to zeros.

Challenge

Arrange the digits 6, 4, 3, 2 in such a way that it forms a number that becomes 3,200 when rounded to the nearest 100.

Exercise 1.3

1. **Round these numbers to the nearest 10. Use the shortcut if you need to.**
   (a) 1,346   (b) 2,388   (c) 10,145
   (d) 92,407   (e) 7,83,093   (f) 11,003

2. **Round these numbers to the nearest 100. Use the shortcut if you need to.**
    (a) 18,649   (b) 75,325   (c) 86,950   (d) 14,910   (e) 4,05,009

3. **Round these numbers to the nearest 1,000. Use the shortcut if you need to.**
    (a) 2,36,473   (b) 3,99,846   (c) 4,09,607   (d) 35,502   (e) 9,77,648

4. **Shade in pencil the 2-digit numbers that can be rounded to 70.**
    Shade the 3-digit numbers that can be rounded to 800.
    Shade the 4-digit numbers that can be rounded to 9,000.

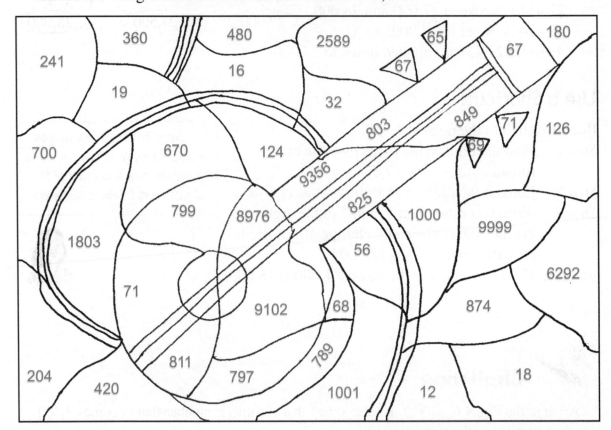

5. **Pretend that you are a newspaper reporter. Rewrite these news headlines by rounding.**
    (a) The municipal corporation spent Rs 5,94,830 on repairing the roads. (nearest 1,000)
    (b) 389 people attended the meeting of coin collectors in the city. (nearest 100)
    (c) The Rajdhani Express was delayed by 5 hours and 15 minutes. (nearest hour)

Number Patterns

1. Consecutive numbers

Numbers that come one after the other on the number line are consecutive numbers.

This pattern has been made by changing 2-digit numbers to 1-digit numbers. Can you see how? Complete the pattern.

1	2	3	4	5	6	7	8	9	10	11	12	13	14	15	16
1	2	3	4	5	6	7	8	9	1	2	3	4	—	—	—

17	18	19	20	21	22	23	24	25	26	27	28	29
—	—	10	2	3	—	—	—	—	—	—	—	—
		1									—	—
		—										

Add only till you see a pattern, then complete.

2. Consecutive even numbers

2	4	6	8	10	12	14	16	18	20	22	24
2	4	6	8	1	3	5	—	—	—	—	—

26	28	30	32	34	36	38	40	42	44	46
—	—	—	—	—	—	—	—	—	—	—
	—									—

3. Consecutive odd numbers

1	3	5	7	9	11	13	15	17	19	21	23	25
—	—	—	—	—	—	—	—	—	—	—	—	—
									—			

4. Adding consecutive odd numbers

$1 + 3 = 4$ $1 + 3 + 5 = 9$

$1 + 3 + 5 + 7 = 16$

Numbers like 4,9,16 are called square numbers because they can be arranged to form a square. Find the next 5 square numbers. Can you find another way to build square numbers?

Try This

Look for a pattern: Can you do it without adding?
$1 + 3 + 5 + 7 + 9 =$ _____
$1 + 3 + 5 + 7 + 9 + 11 =$ _____

Triangle Numbers

3   6   10   _____

Find the next two triangle numbers by drawing the dots. Can you find the following two without drawing dots? Look for a pattern.

Pascal's Triangle

Look for a pattern. Extend the triangle by another two rows.

```
                    1
                 1     1
              1     2     1
           1     3     3     1
        1     4     6     4     1
     1     5    10    10     5     1
  __    __    __    __    __    __
__    __    __    __    __    __    __    __
```

There are many patterns in this triangle. Can you spot at least three?

Project

Complete this famous series of numbers called the Fibonacci Series.
1, 1, 2, 3, 5, 8, 13, __ __ __ __

Use this idea in an addition trick.
Write any two numbers. Say 7 and 4.

⑦
④

Add them: 11 (7+4)
Add the previous two numbers: 15 (4+11)
Add the previous two numbers: 26 (11+15)
Add the previous two numbers: 41 (15+26)
Stop when you have six numbers in a row.
                              Total   ____
Find the total by mutiplying the fifth number, 26 by 4.
26 × 4 = 104.
Check by adding. Try with other numbers.

Roman Numbers

You are familiar with Roman numbers up to 39. Let us look back at the rules of forming Roman numerals and apply it to numbers up to 100.

Remember that the Romans did not have '0'; so they did not use place value. They had seven basic symbols represented by these letters.

Roman Number	I	V	X	L	C	D	M
Hindu-Arabic	1	5	10	50	100	500	1,000

They formed other numbers by combining these letters and following certain rules.

*   Putting a letter **after** one of bigger value means you **add** it.
    (a) 75 = LXXV (50 + 10 + 10 + 5)
    (b) 60 = 50 + 10 = L + X = LX

*   Putting a letter **before** one of bigger value means you **subtract** it.
    (a) 40 = XL (50 – 10)
    (b) 94 = XCIV (100 – 10) + (5 – 1) = 90 + 4

*   A letter can be **repeated** up to a maximum of **three times** only.
    80 = LXXX (50 + 10 + 10 + 10 = 80)

*   When a smaller number that has been made of two letters using the addition/ subtraction rule is combined with a larger number, the **whole of the smaller number is written to the right of the larger one.**
    (a) 59 = LIX
    (b) 74 = 70 + 4 = LXX + IV = LXXIV

*   V and L are never subtracted.
*   I can be subtracted from V and X only.
*   X can be subtracted from L and C only.
*   V and L are never repeated.

Exercise 1.4

1. **Fill in the boxes with Hindu-Arabic numerals.**

XL	X	LXX	XXX	XC	XX	LX	LXXX	C	L
40									

2. **Write the Hindu-Arabic numerals.**
   (a) XXIV   (b) XC   (c) LVII   (d) XLIV   (e) LXXV   (f) LXXXII

3. **Fill in the boxes with Roman numerals.**

41	42	43 XLIII	44	45	46	47	48	49	50
51	52	53	54	55	56	57	58	59	60
61	62	63	64	65	66	67	68	69	70
71	72	73	74	75	76	77	78	79	80
81	82	83	84	85	86	87	88	89	90
91	92	93	94	95	96	97	98	99	100

4. **Compare using <, >, or =.**

   (a) XC ◯ XL   (b) XLIV ◯ LXIV
   (c) XXVII ◯ LX   (d) LVIII ◯ C

5. **Give the answer in Roman numerals.**
   (a) XXV + XL   (b) LXII + XII   (c) LXX + XXX   (d) L – XXXIX

Challenge

Correct this Roman number sentence in three different ways.
(a) By moving one stick
(b) By removing one stick
(c) By not touching any stick

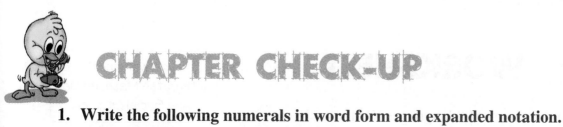

CHAPTER CHECK-UP

1. **Write the following numerals in word form and expanded notation.**
   (a) 11,00,948　　　　　(b) 78,98,001　　　　　(c) 5,67,03,670

2. **Write in figures.**
   (a) Thirty lakh seventy thousand three hundred six
   (b) Four crore seventeen lakh one hundred ninety-five
   (c) Forty-eight lakh three hundred five

3. **Give the place value of the coloured digit.**
   (a) 4,56,7**8**,923　　　　(b) 54,**6**9,345　　　　　(c) **6**,76,13,984

4. **What are the greatest and the smallest 7-digit numbers you can make using the digits 3, 5, 7, 1, 2? (digits may be repeated)**

5. **Write the number after:**　　(a) 79,98,999　　(b) 15,09,999

6. **Write the number before:**　　(a) 5,10,000　　(b) 13,80,970

7. **Compare using >, <, or =.**

   (a) 5,67,98,345 ◯ 5,76,98,435　　　　(b) 67,83,009 ◯ 67,08,900

   (c) LVIII ◯ C　　　　　　　　　　　(d) LXXI ◯ XLIX

8. **Put the commas using the International system and rewrite these statements using the word form of the number.**
   (a) A 15-year-old boy would have lived for 131400 hours.
   (b) 1101395 people travelled by planes this year.

9. **Rewrite these news headlines by rounding.**
   (a) The flight carrying the cricketers from South Africa landed at 8:26 p.m.
       (Round to the nearest half hour.)
   (b) The stolen collection had 13,078 precious stamps and first-day covers.
       (Round to the nearest 1000.)

10. **Write the Roman numerals for:**
    (a) 29　　　　　(b) 12　　　　　(c) 81　　　　　(d) 95

11. **Solve using Roman numerals.**
    (a) XCIII – LXV　　　　　(b) XLVII + XXXIX
    (c) LXXX – XXXI

WORKSHEET

This worksheet integrates Mathematics and Social Studies.

India has more than 1,600 languages. Of these, 18 are officially recognized languages mentioned in our constitution. The table below shows the list of scheduled languages and the number of people speaking each, according to the 1991 census.

Language	Number of People
Assamese	1,30,79,696
Bengali	6,95,95,738
Gujarati	4,06,73,814
Hindi	*33,72,72,114
Kannada	3,27,53,676
Kashmiri	31,76,975
Konkani	17,60,607
Malayalam	3,03,77,176
Manipuri	12,70,216
Marathi	6,24,81,681
Nepali	20,76,645
Oriya	2,80,61,313
Punjabi	2,33,78,744
Sanskrit	49,736
Sindhi	21,22,848
Tamil	5,30,06,368
Telugu	6,60,17,615
Urdu	4,34,06,932

भारत लोक कलाओं की दृष्टि से इतना समृद्ध
संपन्न है कि इसकी थाह लेना मुश्किल है ।
ਇਕ ਦਿਨ ਇਕ ਮੁੰਡਾ ਸਕੂਲ ਤੋਂ ਘਰ ਜਾਂ ਰਿਹਾਂ ਸੀ
ਰਸਤੇ ਵਿਦ ਉਸਨੇ ਵੇਖਿਆਂ ਇਕਮੰਦਮੀ ਜਿਸਦੇ ਪੋਰ
ગુજરાતી શીખવા માટે તથા માબાપને પત્ર લખવા,
માટે આનો ઉપયોગ સરળ રીતે કરી શકાય છે.

1. Which language is spoken by the largest number of people in the country?
2. Which language is spoken by the least number of people?
3. Which language has 9 in the ten lakhs place?
4. What is the place value of 5 in the number of people who speak Tamil?
5. Give the place value of 5 in the number of people who speak Kannada.
6. Write the six most commonly spoken languages in order.

1. Hindi	2.
3.	4.
5.	6.

* This nine-digit number is read as thirty-three crore seventy-two lakh seventy-two thousand one hundred fourteen.

LOOKING BEYOND

Enrichment Time

The ancient Egyptians did not have a place-value system, and neither did they have a symbol for zero. This is how they wrote their numbers

Stick	|	1
Heel bone	∩	10
Coiled rope	ℓ	100
Lotus flower		1000
Pointing finger		10,000
Tadpole		1,00,000
Astonished man		10,00,000

Since they did not have a place value system, they simply combined the symbols and added their values. So they could write the symbols in any order.

18 ∩ | | | | | | | |

350 ℓℓℓ ∩∩∩∩∩

4186 | | | | ℓ ∩∩∩∩∩∩∩∩ | | | | | |

How will you write these numbers using Egyptian numerals?

46

793

5201

Write your age in standard numerals and Egyptian numbers.

Write the year of your birth in standard numerals and Egyptian numerals.

Write the year of our independence in standard numerals and Egyptian numerals.

> I am glad the Indians invented zero. These numbers are too long.

Activity Bag

This game can be played by the class as two teams. Two sets of digit cards from 0 to 9 are to be made. Two sets of place value charts are drawn on the board. A child from each team come up and selects one digit card each and writes the digit he has picked in order starting from the crores place. The card is then placed back in the pile. The next two children come up and do the same thing. The team that make the bigger number wins.

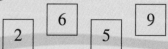

The Four Operations

Looking Back

- When you add, the answer is called the **sum**.

$$4 + 5 = 9 \quad \textbf{Sum}$$

- The answer in subtraction is called the **difference**.

$$9 - 6 = 3 \quad \textbf{Difference}$$

- The numbers that are multiplied are called the **factors** and the answer is called the **product**.

$$7 \times 9 = 63$$

Factors   **Product**

- The terms to be remembered in division are **dividend**, **divisor**, **quotient**, and **remainder**.

$$
\begin{array}{r}
5 \quad \leftarrow \textbf{Quotient} \\
3 \overline{)\ 1\ 6} \quad \leftarrow \textbf{Dividend} \\
-1\ 5 \\
\hline
1 \quad \leftarrow \textbf{Remainder}
\end{array}
$$

Divisor

Solve the following.

1. (a) $17335 + 7998$ (b) $39864 + 23981 + 11125$ (c) $47839 + 12609$
2. (a) $83960 - 5632$ (b) $50039 - 26384$ (c) $60930 - 42983$
3. (a) 7523×4 (b) 568×31 (c) 560×706
4. (a) $2065 \div 9$ (b) $261 \div 28$ (c) $2408 \div 43$

5. **Follow the path to get the answer.**

(a)
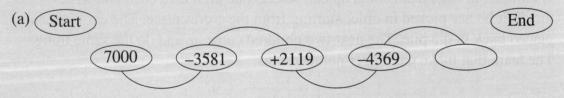

Start — 7000 — −3581 — +2119 — −4369 — End

Addition and Subtraction

Addition

Addition of large numbers is the same as addition of smaller numbers. You **start from the ones place and regroup if necessary.**

```
  L TTh Th  H  T  O            L TTh Th  H  T  O
                                          ②  ①
     ①  ①      ①                  ①  2  7  5  3
     6  1  3  2  7                  2  6  9  3  2
  +  3  9  8  5  5            +  1  4  7  8  4  1
  ─────────────────            ──────────────────
  1  0  1  1  8  2             1  7  7  5  2  6
```

Subtraction

Subtraction of large numbers is the same as subtraction of smaller numbers. You **start from the ones place and regroup if necessary.**
You can check your subtraction with addition.

```
        L TTh Th  H  T  O
                  ⑩
               6  ⓪  14        Check:
     3  5  7̶  1̶  4̶  3          2  0  3  2  9  1
  -  1  5  3  8  5  2        + 1  5  3  8  5  2
  ─────────────────          ──────────────────
     2  0  3  2  9  1         3  5  7  1  4  3
```

Examples with zeros.

(a)
```
     Th  H  T  O
         ⑨  ⑨
      5  ⑩  ⑩  16
      6̶  0̶  0̶  6̶
   -  2  7  5  8
   ─────────────
      3  2  4  8
```

(b)
```
   TTH Th  H  T  O
          ⑭
    1  4̶  10  8  10
    2̶  5̶  0̶  9̶  0̶
    -      8  2  3  4
   ──────────────────
    1  6  8  5  6
```

Use a shortcut!

Subtract: 4000 – 2847
Reduce both numbers by 1 and then **subtract.**
This helps avoid regrouping.

```
(4000 – 1)      3 9 9 9
(2847 – 1)    - 2 8 4 6
              ─────────
                1 1 5 3
```

You can try this method for large numbers also.

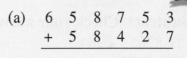

Try This

(a)
```
   6  5  8  7  5  3
 + 5  8  4  2  7
 ─────────────────
```

(b)
```
   2  3  4  6  7  8
 -    6  8  7  5  1
 ─────────────────
```

(c)
```
      7  0  0  0  4
    - 5  4  9  8  7
 ─────────────────
```

(d)
```
      9  0  0  0  0
    - 3  8  6  9  5
 ─────────────────
```

Challenge

Complete the magic square.

44		
99		
58		90

Exercise 2.1

1. **Rewrite in columns using place value and add.**
   (a) 5087 + 26542
   (b) 65875 + 75842
   (c) 45735 + 69046
   (d) 93485 + 48294
   (e) 54567 + 45765 + 12635
   (f) 287635 + 1198
   (g) 51487 + 456 + 239601
   (h) 111321 + 56789 + 45987
   (i) 108162 + 59346 + 18992

2. **Fill in the boxes.**

   (a)
   ```
        2 □ 4 5 6
     + □ 8 □ □ □
     _____
        8 2 0 1 3
   ```

   (b)
   ```
       □ □ 6 □ 2
     +   7 5 □ 5 □
     _____
       □ 4 8 5 0 1
   ```

3. **Subtract. Check your answers with addition.**
   (a) 8765 – 2984
   (b) 93542 – 78645
   (c) 938743 – 78243
   (d) 439235 – 145987
   (e) 30000 – 18603
   (f) 21976 – 8756
   (g) 50001 – 39846
   (h) 20106 – 15302
   (i) 81065 – 21952

4. **Fill in the missing digits.**

   (a)
   ```
       2 4 6 □ 5
     – □ □ □ 3 □
     _____
         5 2 0 4
   ```

   (b)
   ```
       7 □ 7 □ □
     – 1 5 □ 4 6
     _____
       □ 2 2 8 0
   ```

5. **Number tricks.**
   (a) • Choose a 3-digit number with the first digit greater than the third digit.
   • Reverse the digits.
   • Subtract.
   • Reverse the digits.
   • Add.

   ```
        6 7 2
      – 2 7 6
      _____
        3 9 6
      + 6 9 3
      _____
      1 0 8 9
   ```

   Try with these numbers.
   (i)   3 2 1
   (ii) 7 8 2
   (iii) 8 4 4
   (iv) 6 7 5
   (v)   9 8 3
   (vi) Any numbers of your choice.

   What do you notice?

(b) • Write down any three single-digit numbers.

• Make all the possible 2-digit numbers with these digits.

63 64 34 36 46 43

• Add these 2-digit numbers.

63 + 64 + 34 + 36 + 46 + 43 = 286

• Find the sum of the first three single-digit numbers.

6 + 4 + 3 = 13

• Divide.

$$\begin{array}{r} 22 \\ 13\overline{)286} \end{array}$$

Try it with other numbers. What do you find?

Adding and Subtracting with Money

Profit and Loss

It costs me Rs 159 to make this lamp in my factory.

I will sell it for Rs 196 in my shop.

Rs 159 is **the cost price (C.P.)** of the lamp.
Rs 196 is **the selling price (S.P.)** of the lamp.

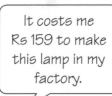

I will earn Rs 37 on each lamp I sell.

Selling Price = Rs 196
Cost Price   = Rs 159
          Rs 37   Profit

When the selling price is more than the cost price the difference is the 'profit'.

This lamp was slightly damaged. So I sold it for Rs 150.

Cost Price   = Rs 159
Selling Price = Rs 150
          Rs 9   Loss

I lost Rs 9 on this lamp

When the cost price is more than the selling price the difference is the "loss".

Say whether it is a loss or a profit.

Cost Price = Rs 237
Selling Price = Rs 292

Cost Price = Rs 286
Selling Price = Rs 268

Cost Price = Rs 305
Selling Price = Rs 340

Cost Price = Rs 329
Selling Price = Rs 319

(b) A second-hand furniture dealer buys a used table for
Rs 3,250. He spends Rs 500 on polishing and repairing it.
If he sells it at Rs 4,000, what is his profit?
   Cost price = Rs 3,250
   Cost of repair = Rs 500
   Total cost to the dealer = cost price + cost of repair
   Total cost price = 3,250 + 500 = Rs 3,750
   Selling price = Rs 4,000
   Selling price is more than cost price.
   Selling Price – Cost Price = Profit
   4,000 – 3,750 = Rs 250
   Answer: The dealer makes a profit of Rs 250 on the table.

To Find the Cost Price

(a) Akshay sold a book for Rs 315 at a loss of Rs 23.
What was the cost of the book?
Selling price = Rs 315
Loss = Rs 23
Cost price = ?
Cost Price = Selling Price + Loss
          = 315 + 23
          = Rs 338
   Answer: The cost price of the book was Rs 338.

(b) Ananya made a profit of Rs 281 on a necklace she sold for Rs 5,389. What had the necklace cost her?
Selling price = Rs 5,389
Profit = Rs 281
Cost price = ?
Cost Price = Selling Price – Profit
= 5389 – 281
= Rs 5108

Answer: The necklace cost Ananya Rs 5,108.

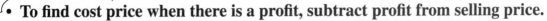

- **To find cost price when there is a profit, subtract profit from selling price.**
- **To find cost price when there is a loss, add loss to selling price.**

To Find the Selling Price

(a) A stamp collector bought a rare stamp for Rs 21,380 and sold it at a profit of Rs 1,500. What was the selling price of the stamp?
Cost price = Rs 21,380
Profit = Rs 1,500
Selling price = ?
Selling Price = Cost Price + Profit
= 21380 + 1500
= Rs 22880

Answer: The collector sold the stamp for Rs 22,880.

(b) Aman bought an encyclopaedia set for Rs 8,350 and sold it after a few years for Rs 550 less than what he paid for it. How much did he sell the set for?
Cost price = Rs 8,350
Loss = Rs 550
Selling price = ?
Selling Price = Cost Price – Loss
= 8350 – 550
= Rs 7800

Answer: He sold the books for Rs 7,800.

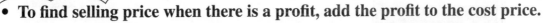

- **To find selling price when there is a profit, add the profit to the cost price.**
- **To find selling price when there is a loss, subtract loss from the cost price.**

1. **Find out the profit or loss in each of these.**

	Cost price	Selling price	Profit/Loss	Amount
(a)	Rs 2,090	Rs 2,100	C.P. < S.P. = Profit	Rs 2100 – Rs 2090 = Rs 10
(b)	Rs 8,395	Rs 8,935		
(c)	Rs 14,060	Rs 14,600		
(d)	Rs 9,319	Rs 9,139		
(e)	Rs 6,250	Rs 6,175		
(f)	Rs 11,190	Rs 11,865		
(g)	Rs 15,000	Rs 14,905		

2. **Complete the table.**

	Selling price	Profit	Loss	Cost price
(a)	Rs 2,385	Rs 195	—	
(b)	Rs 1,900	—	Rs 628	
(c)	Rs 8,630	—	Rs 1,020	
(d)	Rs 11,391	—	Rs 4,060	
(e)	Rs 74,365	Rs 2,315	—	

3. **Complete the table.**

	Cost price	Profit	Loss	Selling price
(a)	Rs 1,095	—	Rs 89	
(b)	Rs 3,586	Rs 369	—	
(c)	Rs 9,980	—	Rs 351	
(d)	Rs 15,381	Rs 1,395	—	
(e)	Rs 3,365	Rs 285	—	

4. (a) A grocer buys goods worth Rs 135 and sells them for Rs 150. What is his profit or loss?

(b) A collector buys a painting for Rs 3,500, but sells it for Rs 2,750. Find the gain or loss.

(c) A calculator that costs Rs 517 is sold at Rs 575. What is the profit that is made?

(d) A used dining set is sold for Rs 9,390. It had been bought for Rs 11,500. What is the loss that is incurred?

(e) A furniture mart buys an old sofa set for Rs 5,380. They spend Rs 1,840 to put new covers on it and sell it for Rs 8,000. What is the profit or loss?

(f)  A dozen books are sold at Rs 648 at a profit of Rs 120. What is the cost price of the books? What is the cost price of one book?

Multiplication

Multiplying by a 2-Digit Number

A factory makes 4375 soaps a day. How many soaps will it make in 47 days?
4375 × 47 = ?

Step 1: Multiply by ones

```
    4 3 7 5
  ×     4 7
  ───────────
  3 0 6 2 5 ──→ (4375 × 7)
```

Step 2: Multiply by tens

```
    4 3 7 5
  ×     4 7
  ───────────
    3 0 6 2 5 ──→ (4375 × 7)
  1 7 5 0 0 0 ──→ (4375 × 40)
```

Step 3: Add

```
      4 3 7 5
    ×     4 7
  ─────────────
    3 0 6 2 5 ──→ (4375 × 7)
  1 7 5 0 0 0 ──→ (4375 × 40)
  ─────────────
  2 0 5 6 2 5 ──→ (4375 × 47)
```

Answer: 2,05,625 soaps will be made in 47 days.

Multiplying by a 3-Digit Number

Step 1: Multiply by ones

```
    6 9 4 5
  ×   4 2 7
  ───────────
  4 8 6 1 5 ──→ (6945 × 7)
```

Step 2: Multiply by tens

```
      6 9 4 5
    ×   4 2 7
  ─────────────
    4 8 6 1 5 ──→ (6945 × 7)
  1 3 8 9 0 0 ──→ (6945 × 20)
```

Step 3: Multiply by hundreds

```
      6 9 4 5
    ×   4 2 7
    4 8 6 1 5 → (6945 × 7)
  1 3 8 9 0 0 → (6945 × 20)
2 7 7 8 0 0 0 → (6945 × 400)
```

Step 4: Add

```
      6 9 4 5
    ×   4 2 7
    4 8 6 1 5
  1 3 8 9 0 0
2 7 7 8 0 0 0
─────────────
2 9 6 5 5 1 5
```

Multiplying with Zeros

When you multiply by multiples of 10, 100, 1000, the product will have **at least the same number of zeros** as the factors. Pay special attention to example (c).

(a) $40 × 70 = 2,800$

(b) $3300 × 900 = 29,70,000$

(c) $6800 × 5000 = 340,00,000$

Try This

(a) $8371 × 97$ (b) $832 × 518$ (c) $4300 × 800$

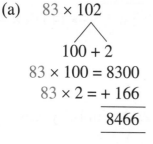

Mental Maths

(a) $83 × 102$

$$100 + 2$$
$$83 × 100 = 8300$$
$$83 × 2 = + 166$$
$$\overline{8466}$$

(b) $19 × 32$

$$20 - 1$$
$$20 × 32 = 640$$
$$1 × 32 = - 32$$
$$\overline{608}$$

Solve.

(a) $48 × 102$ (b) $73 × 102$ (c) $101 × 36$ (d) $101 × 62$

(e) $19 × 34$ (f) $19 × 21$ (g) $24 × 19$ (h) $43 × 19$

Multiplying with Zeros in the Factors

```
    5 3 4 6
  ×   4 0 9
  ─────────
    4 8 1 1 4
    0 0 0 0 0  ←
  2 1 3 8 4 0 0
  ─────────────
  2 1 8 6 5 1 4
```

You do not need to show an extra line for multiplication by 0 tens.

```
    5 3 4 6
  ×   4 0 9
  ─────────
    4 8 1 1 4
  2 1 3 8 4 0 0
  ─────────────
  2 1 8 6 5 1 4
```

Remember

- 2-digit number × 2-digit number cannot give a product of more than 4 digits.
- 3-digit number × 3-digit number cannot give a product of more than 6 digits.
- 3-digit number × 2-digit number cannot give a product of more than 5 digits.

Exercise 2.3

1. **Multiply.**

   (a) 5986×42 (b) 9764×29 (c) 8645×38
   (d) 9307×17 (e) 4876×92 (f) 9752×372
   (g) 4724×466 (h) 5625×635 (i) 403×809
   (j) 5983×604 (k) 4010×506 (l) 60005×908

2. **Multiplication patterns. Calculate only till you see the pattern. Then fill in according to the pattern.**

   (a) $131 \times 11 =$ _____
   $131 \times 111 =$ _____
   $131 \times 1111 =$ _____
   $131 \times 11111 =$ _____
   $131 \times 111111 =$ _____

   (b) $1 \times 9 + 2 =$ _____
   $12 \times 9 + 3 =$ _____
   $123 \times 9 + 4 =$ _____
   $1234 \times 9 + 5 =$ _____
   $12345 \times 9 + 6 =$ _____

   (c) $101 \times 22 =$ _____
   $101 \times 222 =$ _____
   $101 \times 2222 =$ _____
   $101 \times 22222 =$ _____

   (d) $101 \times 33 =$ _____
   $101 \times 333 =$ _____
   $101 \times 3333 =$ _____
   $101 \times 33333 =$ _____

Division

Dividing a 5-Digit Number

A factory produces 59,598 tyres in 23 days. How many tyres does it produce in one day?

- $59598 \div 23$

Method 1

```
              2 5 9 1
    23 ) 5 9 5 9 8
       - 4 6 ↓
           1 3 5
         - 1 1 5 ↓
             2 0 9
           - 2 0 7 ↓
               2 8
             - 2 3
                 5
```

Method 2

```
              2 5 9 1
    23 ) 5 9 5 9 8
       - 4 6 0 0 0  → (23 × 2000)
         1 3 5 9 8
       - 1 1 5 0 0  → (23 × 500)
           2 0 9 8
         - 2 0 7 0  → (23 × 90)
               2 8
             - 2 3  → (23 × 1)
                 5
```

Method 3

In method 2, you can break up the quotient further if you find the numbers too large to multiply with.

```
        1000 + 1000 + 200 + 200 + 100 + 50 + 40 + 1 = 2591
    23 ) 5 9 5 9 8
       - 2 3 0 0 0    (23 × 1000)
         3 6 5 9 8
       - 2 3 0 0 0    (23 × 1000)
         1 3 5 9 8
         - 4 6 0 0    (23 × 200)
           8 9 9 8
         - 4 6 0 0    (23 × 200)
           4 3 9 8
         - 2 3 0 0    (23 × 100)
           2 0 9 8
         - 1 1 5 0    (23 × 50)
             9 4 8
           - 9 2 0    (23 × 40)
               2 8
             - 2 3    (23 × 1)
                 5
```

You can use as many steps as you want. This may seem longer, but you might make fewer mistakes.

Use any method you find easier!

Checking Division

Remember, division is the inverse of multiplication. You can check your division with multiplication.

Quotient × Divisor + Remainder = Dividend

2591 × 23 + 5 = 59598 ← **Right answer!**

 **Exercise 2.4**

1. **Divide and check your answer.**

    (a) 12686 ÷ 51   (b) 49872 ÷ 68   (c) 86243 ÷ 89   (d) 19498 ÷ 49

    (e) 49903 ÷ 72   (f) 48091 ÷ 59   (g) 18468 ÷ 22   (h) 60582 ÷ 87

    (i) 46943 ÷ 58   (j) 53960 ÷ 41   (k) 30045 ÷ 25   (l) 19687 ÷ 35

 ## Problem Solving

Steps

The steps to problem solving will help you think in an organised way and help you decide what to do.

Step 1: Understanding the question

Find the meaning of any word you do not understand. Read the problem slowly twice over, focusing on every word in it. See what the problem is asking for. Repeat it to yourself in your own words in order to make sure you have understood it well.

Step 2: Find the facts

Locate the important information given in the problem. Is all the information you need to solve the problem given in the sum? If you want, write down the important facts.

Step 3: Decide what to do

Think! Do you think you need to add, subtract, multiply, or divide? Do you need to do more than one operation? Is it a multi-step problem? Decide on what to do.

Step 4: Solve the problem

Perform the action you decided upon in the earlier step. Find the answer.

Step 5: **Check back**

This is a very important step. You must read the answer and make sure that:
- It answers the question.
- It makes sense.
- The calculation is correct or it is close to the estimated answer.
- You have used the correct unit.

Let us use the steps of problem-solving to solve this problem.

A shoe factory had an order for 17,024 pairs of boots. If each carton can hold 56 pairs, how many cartons are needed to pack all the boots?

- **Understand the question**
  We need to find the number of cartons that are needed to pack 17,024 pairs of boots.

- **Find the facts**
  17,024 pairs of boots to be packed.
  56 pairs of boots in one carton.

- **Decide what to do**
  Divide 17,024 by 56.

- **Solve the problem**
  $17024 \div 56 = 304$
  Answer: 304 cartons are needed to fit 17,024 pairs of boots.

Check:
- It answers the question.
- It makes sense.
- The calculation is correct.   ($304 \times 56 = 17024$)
- We have used the correct units: 304 cartons

 **Exercise 2.5**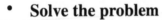

1. **Solve. Keep the steps of problem solving in mind.**
   (a) The Sunshine Club newspaper printed 33,530 copies in a year. Of these 28,395 copies were distributed. How many were not distributed?
   (b) The milometer on a van showed 53,811 km in October. After being used for three months it showed 84,209 km in December. If it had done 21,614 km in October and November, how much did it do in the month of December?

(c)  Sushil's car did 25,384 km in one year, and Suraj's car did 30,001 km in the same year. How many kilometres less did Sushil's car run?

(d) Mr Shenoy had Rs 3,25,765 to buy a new car. He borrowed Rs 1,12,700. How much did the car cost?

(e) Sriram won 75 tournaments. The prize money totalled up to Rs 2,25,000. If he recieved the same amount for every tournament, how much had he earned per tournament?

(f) A school needs 24,510 pencils a year. How many boxes of 25 must the school buy?

(g)  The toy store had 20 boxes of dolls and 25 boxes of teddy bears. Each box holds 24 toys. How many toys did the toy store have in all?

Building Skills—Ask the Question

In this section you will learn how to frame a question when you know the facts and the answer.

Mrs Kumar had Rs 11,250 in the beginning of the month. She spent Rs 5,080 on food and groceries, and Rs 2,110 on school fees, clothes, and entertainment.
Answer: Rs 4,060

On reading the problem and the answer, we realise that the figure of Rs 4,060 is arrived at by first adding the amount spent $(5080 + 2110 = 7190)$ and then subtracting it from the amount at the beginning $(11250 - 7190 = 4060)$.
So the question must be
"How much money was left over with Mrs Kumar?"

Exercise 2.6

1. **The problems given below have the answers but not the question. Write a question that fits the answer.**

   (a) Sahil buys a washing machine for Rs 11,580 and a television set for Rs 15,860.

   _____?

   Answer: Rs 4,280.

   (b) Dhruv sold one second-hand car for Rs 1,10,500 and two second-hand scooters for Rs 7,500 each.

   _____?

   Answer: Rs 1,25,500.

   (c)  A group of 16 students went on a trip. The trip cost them Rs 16,384 altogether.

   _____?

   Answer: Rs 1,024.

   (d) A factory produced 99,400 balloons a month and put them into packets of 50 balloons each.

   _____?

   Answer: 1988 packets.

Challenge

Use the facts given below and build two questions on each.

(a) 7321 mango trees. 5893 apple trees.
(b) 300 books. 25 boxes.

CHAPTER CHECK-UP

1. **Solve.**
   (a) 45673 + 3452 + 456   (b) 34476 + 365432
   (c) 36542 − 27543   (d) 49007 − 25632
   (e) 45631 + 7654 − 36542   (f) 65213 − 4532 − 5643

2. **Multiply.**
   (a) 345 × 907   (b) 4654 × 45   (c) 3487 × 398   (d) 453 × 653

3. **Divide.**
   (a) 5476 ÷ 23   (b) 26590 ÷ 65   (c) 77218 ÷ 35   (d) 65560 ÷ 52

4. **Solve.**
   (a)  A sack holds 560 onions. How many onions can fit in 114 such sacks?

   (b) A tile factory had to pack 1,825 tiles in boxes of 25 tiles each. How many boxes did it need?

   (c) A large library found in the beginning of the month that it had 19,457 books. During the course of the month, it lent 7,654 books but brought 13,871 books. How many books were in the library at the end of the month?

   (d)  A refrigerator is bought for Rs 11,900 and a television set for Rs 12,600. If the refrigerator is sold at a profit of Rs 550 and the television is sold at a loss of Rs 550, what is the selling price of each?

5. **Use the following numbers to build word problems of your own.**
   (a) 348 + 597 − 635   (b) 752 − 574 + 222   (c) 345 ÷ 73   (d) 4590 ÷ 54

6. (a) What number should be added to 78,543 to get 87,653?
   (b) The sum of two numbers is 93,861. If one number is 21,981, what is the other number?
   (c) The product of two numbers is 11,392. If one factor is 64, find the other factor.
   (d) To get a quotient of 56, what number should be divided by 17?

MATHS LAB ACTIVITY

Exploring Multiplication

Objective: To explore multiplication using doubling and halving skills.
Materials Required: Paper and pencils.
Preparation: Students may work in pairs.
Steps:

To solve 26 × 42:

1. One student draws column A and the other student draws column B. Call column A 'half' and column B 'doubles'.

2. Each student then writes the factors as shown. The number in column A is halved and the one in column B is doubled repeatedly. When you have to halve an odd number, ignore the remainder. Both students stop when 1 is reached in column A.

3. Then they cancel all the even numbers from column A and its pair in column B.

4. Next, they add the numbers that are not cancelled from column B only. That gives the product.

This method is also called Russian peasant multiplication.

Try this out:

Try this using Russian peasant multiplication:

| 32 × 53 | A | B |
| | Halves | Doubles |

Example	
To solve 26 × 42:	

A	B
Half	Double
26	42
13	84
6	168
3	336
1	672

A	B
~~26~~	~~42~~
13	84
~~6~~	~~168~~
3	336
1	672

```
  672
  336
+  84
------
 1092
```

26 × 42 = 1092

LOOKING BEYOND

Enrichment Time

Averages

Aditi was skipping in the park. On her first try she skipped 14 times non-stop. Next time she managed to skip 26 times. On her third try she managed 17 skips. Aditi skipped for an **average** of 19 times in each turn.

We find the average by adding all the skips and then dividing the sum by the number of turns.

```
   1 4
   2 6
 + 1 7
 ─────
   5 7
```

57 ÷ 3 = **19**

Try these

1. **This is Mini's skipping score.**

First try	Second try	Third try
25	32	12

   Find her average skips per turn.

2. **These are the mathematics test marks of Sohail. Find the average.**
   23   18   21   25   28

3. **These are the attendance figures of class V. Find the average attendance of the class for five days.**

Monday	Tuesday	Wednesday	Thursday	Friday
31	34	35	32	33

Activity Bag

Large division sums can be done on the board by relay teams of students. The teacher can put up two different sums on the board. A student from each team starts the 'race' and goes back after completing one step of the solution. The next student from the same team will run up and do the next step. The team that first finishes its sum correctly earns 10 points. The second team will get 5 points, if the answer is correct.

Factors and Multiples

Looking Back

Factors are the numbers that are multiplied to give a product. Factors of 10 are 1, 2, 5, 10, because $1 \times 10 = 10$ and $2 \times 5 = 10$.

Factors of a number also divide that number without leaving a remainder.

$12 \div 1 = 12$
$12 \div 2 = 6$ Factors of 12 are
$12 \div 3 = 4$ 1, 2, 3, 4, 6, 12

Common factors of 10 and 12.

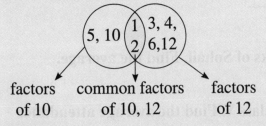

factors   common factors   factors
of 10   of 10, 12   of 12

Multiples are the products you get when you multiply a number by 1, 2, 3, 4, and so on.

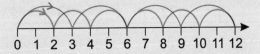

2, 4, 6, 8, 10, 12 are the multiples of 2.
3, 6, 9, 12 are the multiples of 3.
6 and 12 are the **common multiples** of 2 and 3.

Remember

- 1 is a factor of every number. It is also the smallest factor of a number.
- Every number is a factor of itself. It is also the greatest factor of that number.
- The factor of a number is less than or equal to the number.
- Every number (other than 1) has at least 2 factors—1 and the number itself.

Remember

- A number is a multiple of itself.
- Every number is a multiple of 1.
- Every multiple of a number is greater than or equal to the number itself.
- There is no end to the multiples you can get for a particular number.

1. **Write the common factors of:**
   (a) 9 and 15   (b) 18 and 21   (c) 14 and 12   (d) 13 and 65   (e) 27 and 54

2. **Write the first two common multiples of:**
   (a) 5 and 6   (b) 4 and 3   (c) 4 and 8   (d) 2 and 7   (e) 3 and 5

Rules of Divisibility

The rules of divisibility will help you find which numbers divide others without leaving any remainder.

Divisibility by 2, 5, and 10

A number is divisible by	If the last digit is
2	0, 2, 4, 6, 8
5	0, 5
10	0

Number	Divisible by		
	2	5	10
24	✓	✗	✗
40	✓	✓	✓

Divisibility by 3 and 9

A number is divisible by	If the sum of the digits is divisible by
3	3
9	9

Number	Sum of digits	Divisible by	
		3	9
81	8 + 1 = 9	✓	✓
84	8 + 4 = 12	✓	✗

 **Exercise 3.1**

Complete the tables.

1.

	Number	Divisible by		
		2	5	10
(a)	12	✓	✗	✗
(b)	79			
(c)	98			
(d)	65			
(e)	60			
(f)	85			
(g)	38			
(h)	17			

2.

	Number	Divisible by	
		3	9
(a)	42	✓	✗
(b)	63		
(c)	94		
(d)	12		
(e)	54		
(f)	66		
(g)	93		
(h)	37		

Exploring Factors

Put a cross mark (×) in the box to show the factors of the numbers.

The number 1 has only **1** as a factor.

The number 2 has **1** and **2** as factors.

The factors of 3 are **1** and **3**.

Complete the rest.

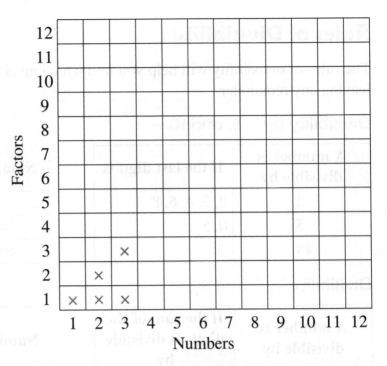

Use the completed grid to answer the following questions.

(a) Complete the table on the right.

(b) Which number is the factor of every number?

(c) How many factors does 10 have?

(d) Which factors are common between 5 and 10?

(e) Which factors are common between 6 and 12? Which is the highest of these?

(f) Which are the numbers that have only two factors? Shade those numbers on the table.

Numbers	Factors
1	1
2	1, 2
3	
4	
5	
6	
7	
8	
9	
10	
11	
12	

Project

Did you know that 6 is called a 'perfect number'?
That is because the factors of 6 (excluding 6 itself) are 1, 2, and 3; $1 + 2 + 3 = 6$. The sum of the factors is also 6.

I am a perfect number.

Find the next perfect number.
(***Hint:*** It is less than 30. Remember, do not include the number itself as a factor while adding.)

Prime and Composite Numbers

Jessica and Joseph are making cubes and cuboids using blocks.
Jessica could make only two cuboidal shapes using 5 blocks.

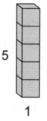

5

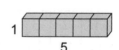

1

1

5

That is because the number 5 has only two factors — 1 and 5 itself.

Numbers more than 1 that have only two factors are called prime numbers.

Use the table on Page 44 to list all the prime numbers up to 12.

Joseph is trying to make the shapes using 4 blocks. He could make three shapes. That is because 4 has three factors — 1, 2, and 4.

4

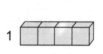

1

2

1

4

2

Numbers more than 1 that have more than two factors are called composite numbers.

Use the table on Page 44 to list the composite numbers up to 12.

The number 1 has only one factor. It is neither prime nor composite.

Try This

1. Make rectangles on the grid to show the factors of 13. How many rectangles could you make? Is it prime or composite?
2. Do the same with 14. Is it prime or composite?

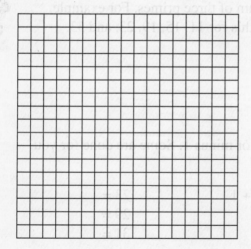

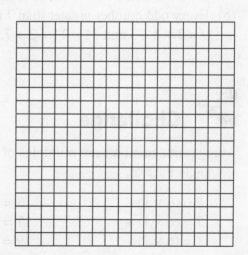

Primes between 1 and 100

A Greek mathematician, named Eratosthenes, long ago found a simple method of locating prime numbers from 1 to 100. This is called the Sieve of Eratosthenes.

1	2	3	4	5	6	7	8	9	10
11	12	13	14	15	16	17	18	19	20
21	22	23	24	25	26	27	28	29	30
31	32	33	34	35	36	37	38	39	40
41	42	43	44	45	46	47	48	49	50
51	52	53	54	55	56	57	58	59	60
61	62	63	64	65	66	67	68	69	70
71	72	73	74	75	76	77	78	79	80
81	82	83	84	85	86	87	88	89	90
91	92	93	94	95	96	97	98	99	100

- Cross 1 as it is neither prime nor composite.
- Leave 2 as it is a prime number but cross out all the multiples of 2.
- Leave 3 as it is prime, but cross out all its multiples.
- Leave 5, but cross out all its multiples.
- Leave 7, but cross out all its multiples.

All the numbers that are not crossed out are prime numbers.

Use the grid above to answer these questions.
(a) List all the prime numbers from 1 to 100.
(b) Which is the only even prime number?
(c) Which are the only prime numbers that end with 2 and 5?
(d) Which is the greatest prime number less than 100?

Project

(a) Every even number except 2 is the sum of two primes. For example, $8 = 5 + 3$ and $14 = 7 + 7$. Prove this for 12, 18, 24, 32, and 40.
(b) Every odd number greater than 7 is the sum of three primes. For example, $9 = 3 + 3 + 3$ and $21 = 11 + 3 + 7$. Prove this for 11, 15, 19, 23, and 33.

Challenge

Many prime numbers are multiples of 6, plus or minus 1. Some are done for you. complete the rest.

$5 = (6 \times 1) - 1$ $13 = (6 \times 2) + 1$ $23 =$

$7 = (6 \times 1) + 1$ $17 =$ $29 =$

$11 = (6 \times 2) - 1$ $19 =$ $31 =$

Prime Factorisation

All composite numbers can be broken up into their factors.

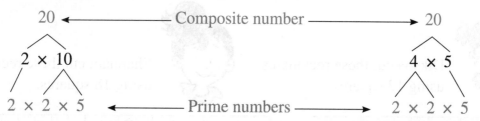

When the factors are all prime, it is called the **prime factorisation** of the number. Prime factorisation of 20 = 2 × 2 × 5.

Prime Factorisation Method

(a) Find the prime factors of 64.

Step 1:   Start with the smallest prime factor of 64.

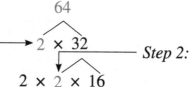

64

2 × 32

2 × 2 × 16

2 × 2 × 2 × 8

2 × 2 × 2 × 2 × 4

2 × 2 × 2 × 2 × 2 × 2

Step 2:   Next find the smallest prime factor of 32.

Step 3:   Continue to find the smallest prime factor at every step.

Stop when the last row has only prime numbers.

Check: 2 × 2 × 2 × 2 × 2 × 2 = 64

(b) Find the prime factors of 56 using prime factorisation method.

$$56 = 2 \times 28$$
$$= 2 \times 2 \times 14$$
$$= 2 \times 2 \times 2 \times 7$$

Answer: The prime factorisation of 56 = 2 × 2 × 2 × 7.

 **Exercise 3.2**

1. **Use prime factorisation to find the prime factors of these composite numbers.**

(a) 51	(b) 60	(c) 90	(d) 32	(e) 24	(f) 63
(g) 81	(h) 72	(i) 28	(j) 88	(k) 62	(l) 45
(m) 56	(n) 44	(o) 65	(p) 70	(q) 87	(r) 94

Highest Common Factor

Diksha and Shabnam were exploring number rectangles.

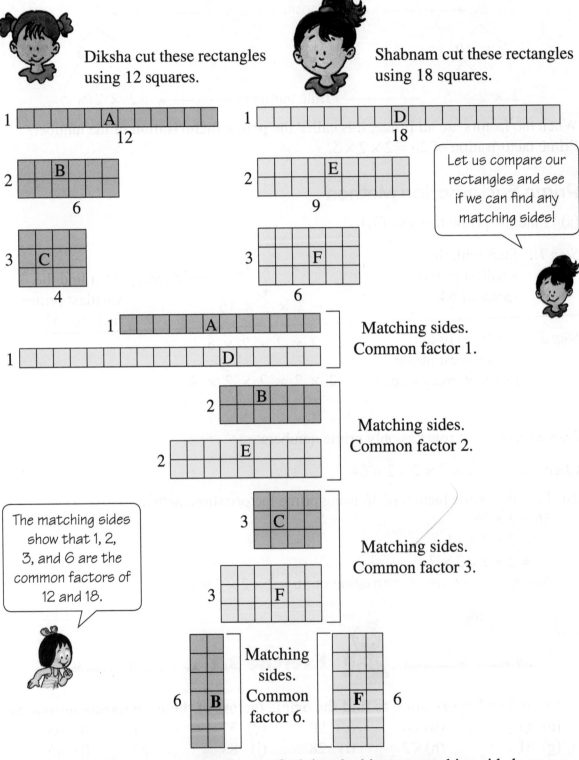

Diksha cut these rectangles using 12 squares.

Shabnam cut these rectangles using 18 squares.

Let us compare our rectangles and see if we can find any matching sides!

Matching sides. Common factor 1.

Matching sides. Common factor 2.

The matching sides show that 1, 2, 3, and 6 are the common factors of 12 and 18.

Matching sides. Common factor 3.

Matching sides. Common factor 6.

If you look at all the matching sides, we find that the biggest matching side between the two sets of rectangles is the side that shows the factor 6. We call this **highest common factor (HCF)** of 12 and 18.

To find HCF using factors

Factors of 12: 1, 2, 3, 4, 6, 12
Factors of 18: 1, 2, 3, 6, 9, 18

Factors of 12   **Factors of 18**

**Common factors of
12 and 18**

Factors of 12   **Factors of 18**

The common factors of 12 and 18 are 1, 2, 3, and 6. The **highest common factor (HCF)** of 12 and 18 is 6.

The HCF of two numbers is the greatest number that divides both the numbers without leaving any remainder.

To find HCF using prime factorisation

(a) Let us find the HCF of 24 and 32 using prime factorisation.

   Step 1: Do the **prime factorisation** of the numbers.

   $24 = 2 \times 2 \times 2 \times 3$
   $32 = 2 \times 2 \times 2 \times 2 \times 2$

   Step 2: Find the common factors. ⟶ Common factors are 2, 2, 2

   Step 3: **Multiply** the common factors. ⟶ $2 \times 2 \times 2 = 8$
   Answer: HCF of 24 and 32 is 8.

(b) Find the HCF of 10, 12, and 15.
   $10 = 2 \times 5$
   $12 = 2 \times 2 \times 3$
   $15 = 3 \times 5$
   There is no common prime factor here; so the HCF is 1.
   Answer: HCF of 10, 12, and 15, is 1.

Common Mistake!

HCF of 10, 12, and 15 = ?
$10 = 2 \times 5$
$12 = 2 \times 2 \times 3$
$15 = 3 \times 5$
HCF = $2 \times 3 \times 5 = 30$ ✗
HCF = 1 ✓

Remember

The HCF of given numbers cannot be bigger than any one of the numbers.

1. **Find the common factors of these numbers. Then find their HCF.**

Numbers		Factors	Common factors	Highest common factor
(a)	9			
	15			
(b)	4			
	18			
(c)	28			
	32			
(d)	40			
	24			
(e)	66			
	44			

2. **Find the HCF of these numbers using the prime factorisation method.**

   (a) 6, 10   (b) 16, 8   (c) 15, 25   (d) 16, 48
   (e) 28, 36   (f) 36, 45   (g) 27, 36   (h) 28, 33
   (i) 6, 15, 45   (j) 15, 36 45   (k) 6, 10, 28   (l) 4, 24, 48
   (m) 6, 10, 15   (n) 3, 24, 15   (o) 15, 20, 35   (p) 16, 18, 24

Lowest Common Multiple

Amudha was making a special 'THANK YOU' poster to put up in class for Teacher's Day.

T	H	A	N	K	T	H	A	N	K	T	H	A	N	K
Y	O	U	Y	O	U	Y	O	U	Y	O	U	Y	O	U

This was the shortest possible poster she could make with complete words. There are 15 boxes in each row.
We could have found this using another method.

THANK – 5 letters   YOU – 3 letters

Multiples of 5 – 5, 10, 15, 20, 25, 30, ...
Multiples of 3 – 3, 6, 9, 12, 15, 18, 21, 24, 27, 30, ...

Common multiples of 3 and 5 are 15, 30, and so on.
Lowest common multiple of 3 and 15 is $\boxed{15}$

Therefore the shortest possible poster that could have been made was 15 squares long.

Try This

Make a poster which says 'BEST WISHES'. What is the length of the shortest poster you can make?

Words   No. of letters   Multiples
BEST   4
WISHES   6

Common multiples ___ ___ ___
Lowest common multiple ___
Check to see if you are right.

B	E	S	T	B										
W	I	S	H	E	S									

Look at the number line that shows the multiples of 2 on top and the multiples of 3 below:

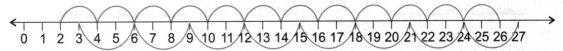

The places where the two multiples meet are the common multiples.
They are 6, 12, 18, ...
The lowest of these is the first place where both multiples meet, that is at 6.
6 is the **lowest common multiple (LCM)** of 2 and 3.

The LCM of two or more numbers is the smallest number that can be divided by those numbers without leaving a remainder.

To find LCM by prime factorisation

(a) Let us find the LCM of 20 and 16 by prime factorisation.

Step 1: Find the prime factors of 20. ⟶ ② × ②   × 5

Step 2: Find the prime factors of 16. ⟶ ② × ② × 2 × 2

Step 3: Multiply the common factors and the
factors that are not common. ⟶ 2 × 2 × 2 × 2 × 5 = 80

Answer: LCM = 80.

(b) Find the LCM of 18, 30, and 50.

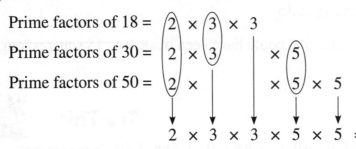

Prime factors of 18 = 2 × 3 × 3

Prime factors of 30 = 2 × 3 × 5

Prime factors of 50 = 2 × × 5 × 5

2 × 3 × 3 × 5 × 5 = 450

Answer: LCM = 450.

Challenge

Four friends go to a park for a walk in the morning. Praneeta goes every day, Sunita goes only every second day, Sheila goes only every third day, and Ramila goes only every fourth day. If Praneeta starts her walk on October 01, Sunita on October 02, Sheila on October 03, and Ramila on October 04, on which date will all four friends meet at the park?

Exercise 3.4

1. **First find 6 multiples of each of these numbers, and then find 3 common multiples. Finally, find the LCM.**

Numbers		Multiples	Common multiples	LCM
(a)	6			
	9			
(b)	5			
	10			
(c)	3			
	6			
	2			

> Of two numbers, if one is a multiple of the other, the greater number is the LCM.

2. **Find the LCM of these numbers using the prime factorisation method.**

   (a) 18, 32   (b) 13, 39   (c) 42, 65   (d) 12, 15   (e) 38, 72
   (f) 24, 56   (g) 25, 90   (h) 63, 81   (i) 18, 63   (j) 96, 84
   (k) 72, 32   (l) 81, 64   (m) 30, 45   (n) 15, 60   (o) 16, 12, 32
   (p) 10, 15, 20   (q) 15, 30, 90   (r) 42, 36, 18   (s) 12, 15, 45   (t) 18, 63, 27

CHAPTER CHECK-UP

1. Complete the HCF chart. Some are done for you.

HCF	6	12	15	18	24	30	36
3	3						
6							
9				9			
12							
24						6	

2. Complete the LCM chart. Some are done for you.

LCM	1	2	3	4	5	6	7	8	9
1	1								
2		2							
3									
4						12			
5									
6									
7									
8		8							
9									9

3. Find the prime factors in each of the following.
   (a) 48   (b) 39   (c) 60   (d) 87   (e) 92

4. Find the HCF using prime factorisation.
   (a) 16, 24   (b) 14, 56   (c) 36, 28   (d) 14, 28
   (e) 13, 24, 86   (f) 42, 72, 18   (g) 56, 14, 28   (h) 16, 32, 40

5. Find the LCM using prime factorisation.
   (a) 36, 42   (b) 40, 75   (c) 39, 78   (d) 38, 14
   (e) 21, 14, 42   (f) 28, 32, 16   (g) 11, 24, 44   (h) 34, 52, 72

WORKSHEET

Prime Designs

Draw a circle with 12 dots equally spaced out.

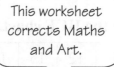

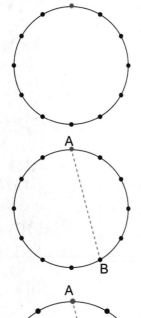

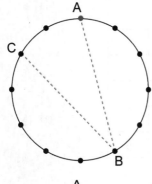

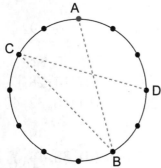

- Since the circle has 12 dots, take any prime number that is not a factor of 12. Let us take 5.
- Mark the top most dot in red. Call it A.
- Count 5 dots **after** the red dot and mark it as B.
- Join A and B.
- Count 5 dots after B and call it C. Join B and C.
- Continue like this till you reach the dot L
- Join L and A.
- Erase all the letters outside the circle.
- What do you get?

You can do this activity with any number of dots on the circle. To join the dots, make sure that you choose **a prime number that is not a factor** of the number of dots.

Keeping in Touch

(a) 35921 + 16847   (b) 90101 – 23462
(c) 843 × 207   (d) 73120 ÷ 56

MATHS LAB ACTIVITY

Lowest Common Multiple

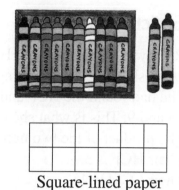

Objective: To explore the concept of LCM.

Materials Required: Square-lined paper, crayons of two colours

Preparation: Students work in pairs using coloured rectangles of 3 squares length and 4 squares length to represent bricks.

Square-lined paper

Method:

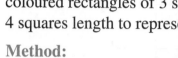

Steps:

1. The students use the square-lined paper and crayons to colour (build) a brick wall. The wall is made of two layers only. The lower layer has bricks of 4 squares only, and the upper layer has bricks of 3 squares only.
2. The students colour the bricks one at a time (taking turns) to make the **shortest** wall possible with no brick jutting out. What is the length of the wall?
3. They then discuss and record their observation.

Record the activity:

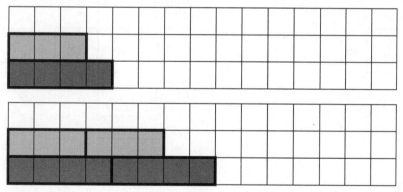

Try this out:

Repeat the same activity with bricks of length 4 squares and 5 squares.

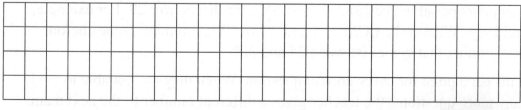

LOOKING BEYOND

Enrichment Time

Rhea was working on her HCF–LCM chapter when she noticed something interesting.
She had found the HCF and LCM of the numbers 15 and 9. This is what she observed.

The product of the two numbers is $15 \times 9 = 135$.
Their HCF is 3.
Their LCM is 45.
The product of the HCF and LCM is
$3 \times 45 = 135$

HCF	3

15	×	9	=	135

LCM	45

=

135

The product of the numbers is equal to the product of their HCF and LCM.

Fill in the empty boxes.

(a) Numbers 6 and 8.
    HCF = _____
    LCM = _____

HCF	

6	×	8	=	

LCM	

=

(b) Numbers 12 and 18.
    HCF = _____
    LCM = _____

HCF	

12	×	18	=	

LCM	

=

Activity Bag

Play 'The Answer is'. The class is divided into two teams. The teacher gives one team a number saying 'The answer is 28, what is the question?' The team has to give as many possible questions that would give the answer 28. For example, they could say 'What is the LCM of 4 and 7?' or 'What number comes before the prime number that comes between 25 and 30?'

The teams get a point for every correct question. When they are not able to frame any more questions, the teacher gives a different number to the next team. The team with maximum points wins.

TEST YOUR SKILLS*

1. What are the greatest and smallest 7-digit numbers you can make with 0, 6, 2, 9, and 5?

2. Write the Roman numeral for 92.

3. 5 31 56 760 ◯ 5 13 65 760 (use > or <)

4. Round 4, 09, 563 to the nearest 1000.

5. Write the number 1 01 11 302 using the International system.

6. (a) 53294 + 68142 + 1398
   (b) 60215 − 31425 − 9399
   (c) 239 × 658
   (d) 92618 ÷ 83

7. **Use prime factorisation to find:**
   (a) HCF of
       (i) 18, 54   (ii) 36, 16, 28
   (b) LCM of
       (i) 16, 12, 18   (ii) 76, 39

8.  Class V collects Rs 2050 to put up a food stall at the school fete. They collect Rs 3185 at the stall. How much profit did they make?

9. A man sells his computer for Rs 12,385 at a loss of Rs 4389. What was the original cost of the computer?

* This is for Chapters 1, 2, and 3.

Fractions

 Looking Back

A fraction shows part of a whole. A whole can be a region or a collection.

   $\frac{1}{4}$ $\dfrac{\text{Numerator}}{\text{Denominator}}$  $\frac{3}{5}$

> A fraction that has 1 as the numerator is called a unit fraction.

You are familiar with the following types of fractions.

Like fractions: $\frac{3}{7}, \frac{5}{7}, \frac{1}{7}$ Proper fractions: $\frac{1}{8}, \frac{4}{9}, \frac{6}{11}$

Unlike Fractions: $\frac{4}{7}, \frac{3}{10}, \frac{5}{9}$ Improper Fractions: $\frac{5}{2}, \frac{12}{7}, \frac{8}{3}$

1. **Compare the following like fractions using < or >.**

   (a) $\frac{7}{12} \bigcirc \frac{9}{12}$ (b) $\frac{8}{11} \bigcirc \frac{3}{11}$ (c) $\frac{6}{8} \bigcirc \frac{3}{8}$

2. (a) Change into mixed fractions. (i) $\frac{17}{8}$ (ii) $\frac{26}{13}$

   (b) Change into improper fractions. (i) $2\frac{3}{7}$ (ii) $5\frac{8}{9}$

3. **Colour to show equivalent fractions.**

   (a)   (b)

   $\frac{1}{2} = \frac{2}{4}$ $\frac{2}{8} = \frac{1}{4}$

4. Of the Rs 2400 Mr Krishnan earned, he spent $\frac{3}{8}$ on food, $\frac{1}{3}$ on taxes and $\frac{1}{6}$ on other expenses. Find out how much all this is in rupees. Then find out how much he saved.

Finding Equivalent Fractions

Mrs Shah baked 2 cakes of the same size.

 She divided one cake into 2 equal parts and gave $\frac{1}{2}$ to her daughter.

 She divided the other cake into 4 equal parts and gave $\frac{2}{4}$ to her son.

$\frac{1}{2} = \frac{2}{4}$ 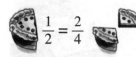 Both got the same amount.

We can find equivalent fractions by multiplying the numerator and denominator by the same number.

(a) $\frac{1 \,(\times 4)}{2 \,(\times 4)} = \frac{4}{8}$

(b) $\frac{2 \,(\times 2)}{3 \,(\times 2)} = \frac{4}{6}$

We can also find equivalent fractions by dividing the numerator and denominator by the same number.

(a) 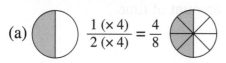 Piyush painted $\frac{4}{6}$ of a wall.

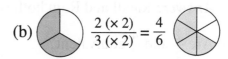 Pratibha painted $\frac{2}{3}$ of another wall.

Take Piyush's fraction $\frac{4}{6}$ and divide both the numerator and the denominator by any common factor other than 1.

$\frac{4 \,(\div 2)}{6 \,(\div 2)} = \frac{2}{3}$

Both Piyush and Pratibha painted the same amount.

(b) $\frac{6 \,(\div 3)}{9 \,(\div 3)} = \frac{2}{3}$

$\frac{14 \,(\div 7)}{21 \,(\div 7)} = \frac{2}{3}$

$\frac{6}{9} = \frac{14}{21} = \frac{2}{3}$

(c) $\frac{3}{7} = \frac{15}{\boxed{?}}$

Think: $3 \times ? = 15$
$3 \times 5 = 15$
$7 \times 5 = ?$

$\frac{3 \,(\times 5)}{7 \,(\times 5)} = \frac{15}{35}$

$\frac{3}{7} = \frac{15}{35}$

(d) $\frac{18}{45} = \frac{\boxed{?}}{5}$

Think: $45 \div ? = 5$
$45 \div 9 = 5$
$18 \div 9 = ?$

$\frac{18 \,(\div 9)}{45 \,(\div 9)} = \frac{2}{5}$

$\frac{18}{45} = \frac{2}{5}$

Checking Equivalent Fractions

(a) Rahul studied for $\frac{2}{5}$ of an hour and Raju studied for $\frac{6}{15}$ of an hour. Did they both study for the same amount of time?

If we want to check whether two fractions are equivalent, we must **cross-multiply**.

$$\frac{2}{5} \times \frac{6}{15} \longrightarrow 5 \times 6 = 30$$
$$\longrightarrow 2 \times 15 = 30$$

Since the cross-products are equal, the fractions are equivalent.

Answer: Rahul and Raju both studied for the same amount of time.

(b) Are $\frac{2}{5}$ and $\frac{4}{7}$ equivalent?

$$\frac{2}{5} \times \frac{4}{7} \longrightarrow 5 \times 4 = 20$$
$$\longrightarrow 2 \times 7 = 14$$

Since the cross-products are not equal, the fractions are not equivalent.

Answer: $\frac{2}{5}$ and $\frac{4}{7}$ are not equivalent.

Exercise 4.1

1. **Multiply the numerator and the denominator by 2 in each of these to get an equivalent fraction.**

   (a) $\frac{1}{2}$ (b) $\frac{2}{3}$ (c) $\frac{1}{5}$ (d) $\frac{2}{5}$ (e) $\frac{1}{3}$ (f) $\frac{2}{7}$

2. **Multiply the numerator and the denominator by 3 in each of these to get an equivalent fraction.**

   (a) $\frac{1}{4}$ (b) $\frac{3}{5}$ (c) $\frac{1}{6}$ (d) $\frac{1}{5}$ (e) $\frac{2}{5}$ (f) $\frac{4}{5}$

3. **Multiply the numerator and the denominator by 2, 3, and 4 in each of these to get a set of equivalent fractions.** *The first one has been done for you.*

   (a) $\frac{1}{5} = \frac{2}{10} = \frac{3}{15} = \frac{4}{20}$ (b) $\frac{1}{4}$ (c) $\frac{2}{3}$ (d) $\frac{2}{5}$ (e) $\frac{3}{4}$

4. **Fill in the boxes.**

   (a) $\frac{1}{3} = \frac{2}{\Box} = \frac{\Box}{9} = \frac{\Box}{12}$ (b) $\frac{5}{6} = \frac{\Box}{12} = \frac{15}{\Box} = \frac{20}{\Box}$

5. **Cross-multiply to find whether the fractions are equivalent. Write E if they are and NE if they are not.**

(a) $\dfrac{4}{5}$ $\dfrac{8}{10}$ (b) $\dfrac{6}{9}$ $\dfrac{3}{2}$ (c) $\dfrac{1}{6}$ $\dfrac{2}{3}$

(d) $\dfrac{4}{5}$ $\dfrac{6}{8}$ (e) $\dfrac{2}{6}$ $\dfrac{4}{12}$ (f) $\dfrac{2}{4}$ $\dfrac{3}{6}$

6. **Divide by a common factor to get an equivalent fraction.**

(a) $\dfrac{6}{24}$ (b) $\dfrac{14}{49}$ (c) $\dfrac{28}{32}$

(d) $\dfrac{10}{30}$ (e) $\dfrac{17}{34}$ (f) $\dfrac{88}{120}$

7. **Fill in the empty boxes.**

(a) $\dfrac{2}{5} = \dfrac{\square}{15}$ (b) $\dfrac{5}{7} = \dfrac{10}{\square}$ (c) $\dfrac{\square}{5} = \dfrac{20}{25}$ (d) $\dfrac{5}{\square} = \dfrac{15}{21}$

(e) $\dfrac{8}{15} = \dfrac{40}{\square}$ (f) $\dfrac{42}{\square} = \dfrac{6}{7}$ (g) $\dfrac{\square}{7} = \dfrac{15}{35}$ (h) $\dfrac{3}{\square} = \dfrac{18}{24}$

Reducing a Fraction to its Lowest Term

When you multiply both the terms of a fraction by the same number, you get an equivalent fraction.

$$\dfrac{1\,(\times 2)}{2\,(\times 2)} = \dfrac{2}{4} \quad \text{or} \quad \dfrac{1\,(\times 3)}{2\,(\times 3)} = \dfrac{3}{6}$$

$\dfrac{1}{2}, \dfrac{2}{4}, \dfrac{3}{6}$ are all equivalent fractions but $\dfrac{1}{2}$ is the fraction in its **lowest term**.

A fraction is in the lowest term when the only common factor between the numerator and the denominator is 1.

A fraction can be reduced to its lowest terms by the following methods.

Abu and Amina were trying to reduce the fraction $\dfrac{18}{30}$ to its lowest term.

Amina's way

$$\dfrac{18\,(\div 2)}{30\,(\div 2)} = \dfrac{9\,(\div 3)}{15\,(\div 3)} = \dfrac{3}{5}$$

$\dfrac{3}{5}$ is the lowest term of the fraction.

> Keep dividing the numerator and the denominator by the same number till you cannot divide further.

Abu's way

The HCF of 18 and 30 is 6.
Divide both the terms by 6.

$$\frac{18 \ (\div 6)}{30 \ (\div 6)} = \frac{3}{5}$$

$\frac{3}{5}$ is the lowest term fraction of $\frac{18}{30}$.

> You can also reduce a given fraction to its lowest term in just one step by **finding the HCF** of both the terms and then dividing by it.

> Do you prefer Abu's way or Amina's way?

 **Exercise 4.2**

1. **Reduce the fraction to its lowest term in each of the following.**

   (a) $\frac{14 \ (\div 7)}{21 \ (\div 7)}$ (b) $\frac{9 \ (\div 3)}{12 \ (\div 3)}$ (c) $\frac{10 \ (\div 5)}{15 \ (\div 5)}$ (d) $\frac{12 \ (\div 4)}{16 \ (\div 4)}$ (e) $\frac{18 \ (\div 9)}{27 \ (\div 9)}$ (f) $\frac{6 \ (\div 2)}{10 \ (\div 2)}$

2. **Reduce the following fractions to their lowest terms.**

   (a) $\frac{2}{6}$ (b) $\frac{4}{8}$ (c) $\frac{6}{8}$ (d) $\frac{4}{6}$ (e) $\frac{12}{15}$ (f) $\frac{12}{18}$ (g) $\frac{16}{20}$ (h) $\frac{7}{35}$

3. **Circle the fractions in its lowest terms.**

   (a) $\frac{3}{15}$ (b) $\frac{4}{12}$ (c) $\frac{1}{5}$ (d) $\frac{2}{11}$ (e) $\frac{3}{5}$ (f) $\frac{5}{7}$ (g) $\frac{6}{8}$ (h) $\frac{9}{18}$

Project

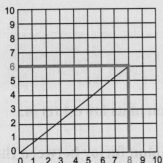

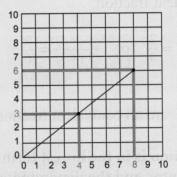

(a) Take any fraction that is not in its lowest term and represent it on a square-lined paper. Here the fraction $\frac{6}{8}$ is shown with blue lines.

(b) Use a ruler to draw a line from 0 to the opposite corner of the rectangle.

(c) Which other corner does the line cut through?

(d) Create a red rectangle there.

(e) What fraction does the red rectangle represent? $\frac{3}{4}$

(f) What can you say about this fraction?

Try this with (a) $\frac{2}{6}$, (b) $\frac{6}{9}$, and (c) $\frac{8}{10}$ in your notebook.

Comparing Fractions

Like Fractions

(a) Arun, Aman, and Bittoo tried out for the long jump at the school sports meet. These are the lengths they jumped. Whose jump was the longest? Whose was the shortest?

  Arun jumped $\frac{7}{10}$ of the length.

 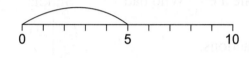 Aman jumped $\frac{5}{10}$ of the length.

 Bittoo jumped $\frac{8}{10}$ of the length.

Like fractions are easy to compare since their denominators are the same.
We compare the numerators and the greater numerator is the greater fraction.

Bittoo   Arun   Aman

$$\frac{8}{10} \quad > \quad \frac{7}{10} \quad > \quad \frac{5}{10}$$

Bittoo's jump was the longest and Aman's was the shortest.

(b) Rearrange these fractions in ascending order.

$$\frac{5}{13} \quad \frac{2}{13} \quad \frac{6}{13} \quad \frac{11}{13} \quad \frac{1}{13} \qquad\qquad \frac{1}{13} < \frac{2}{13} < \frac{5}{13} < \frac{6}{13} < \frac{11}{13}$$

Unlike Fractions

To compare unlike fractions we must first change them to like fractions.

Fractions with the same numerator.

(a) Shikha ate $\frac{1}{3}$ of her pizza. Susie ate $\frac{1}{4}$ of her pizza.

Who ate more?

Find equivalent fractions of $\frac{1}{3}$ and $\frac{1}{4}$ such that they

are **like fractions.**

$$\frac{1}{3} = \frac{2}{6} = \frac{3}{9} = \frac{4}{12} \quad \frac{1}{4} = \frac{2}{8} = \frac{3}{12}$$

$$\frac{4}{12} > \frac{3}{12} \qquad \textit{Answer: } \frac{1}{3} > \frac{2}{6}; \text{ so Shikha ate more.}$$

Shikha   Susie

$\frac{1}{3}$ $\frac{1}{4}$

$\frac{4}{12}$ > $\frac{3}{12}$

63

In unlike fractions with the same numerator, the fraction with the greater denominator is the smaller fraction.

(a) Rearrange these fractions in descending order.

$$\frac{5}{6}, \frac{5}{12}, \frac{5}{7}, \frac{5}{16}, \frac{5}{13} \qquad \frac{5}{6} > \frac{5}{7} > \frac{5}{12} > \frac{5}{13} > \frac{5}{16}$$

(b) Rearrange these fractions in ascending order.

$$\frac{7}{11}, \frac{7}{17}, \frac{7}{9}, \frac{7}{15}, \frac{7}{10} \qquad \frac{7}{17} < \frac{7}{15} < \frac{7}{11} < \frac{7}{10} < \frac{7}{9}$$

Fractions with different numerators

(b) Later Shikha ate $\frac{3}{4}$ of her pizza and Susie ate $\frac{5}{6}$. Who had eaten more?

Change the unlike fractions into like fractions.

$$\frac{3}{4} = \frac{6}{8} = \frac{9}{12} \qquad\qquad \frac{5}{6} = \frac{10}{12}$$

$$\frac{9}{12} < \frac{10}{12}$$

Answer: $\frac{3}{4} < \frac{5}{6}$; so Susie ate more.

Shikha   Susie

$$\frac{3}{4} \qquad\qquad \frac{5}{6}$$

$$\frac{9}{12} \qquad < \qquad \frac{10}{12}$$

Use a shortcut!

$$\frac{2}{3} \enspace ? \enspace \frac{4}{5}$$

- **Find** the LCM of 3 and 5. The LCM is 15.
- **Convert** the given fractions into equivalent fractions with denominator 15.

> Find the factor that gives 15 as a denominator in both the fractions.

$$\frac{2 \,(\times 5)}{3 \,(\times 5)} = \frac{10}{15} \qquad\qquad \frac{4 \,(\times 3)}{5 \,(\times 3)} = \frac{12}{15}$$

$$\frac{10}{15} < \frac{12}{15}$$

Answer: $\frac{2}{3} < \frac{4}{5}$

(a) Rearrange the following fractions into both ascending and descending order.

$$\frac{1}{2}, \frac{2}{3}, \frac{5}{6}, \frac{3}{8}$$

Convert them into like fractions.
LCM of denominators 2, 3, 6, 8 = 24

$$\frac{1}{2} = \frac{1 \times 12}{2 \times 12} = \frac{12}{24} \qquad \frac{2}{3} = \frac{2 \times 8}{3 \times 8} = \frac{16}{24} \qquad \frac{5}{6} = \frac{5 \times 4}{6 \times 4} = \frac{20}{24} \qquad \frac{3}{8} = \frac{3 \times 3}{8 \times 3} = \frac{9}{24}$$

In ascending order

$$\frac{9}{24}, \frac{12}{24}, \frac{16}{24}, \frac{20}{24}$$

$$\frac{3}{8} < \frac{1}{2} < \frac{2}{3} < \frac{5}{6}$$

In descending order

$$\frac{20}{24}, \frac{16}{24}, \frac{12}{24}, \frac{9}{24}$$

$$\frac{5}{6} > \frac{2}{3} > \frac{1}{2} > \frac{3}{8}$$

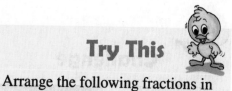

Try This

Arrange the following fractions in ascending and descending orders.

$$\frac{3}{8}, \frac{1}{4}, \frac{5}{8}, \frac{5}{6}$$

Exercise 4.3

1. **Put the >, <, or = signs without changing into equivalent fractions. Apply the rules you have learnt so far.**

   (a) $\frac{2}{5} \bigcirc \frac{2}{7}$ (b) $\frac{1}{7} \bigcirc \frac{1}{9}$ (c) $\frac{5}{12} \bigcirc \frac{5}{11}$ (d) $\frac{1}{11} \bigcirc \frac{1}{13}$

   (e) $\frac{3}{13} \bigcirc \frac{3}{7}$ (f) $\frac{6}{15} \bigcirc \frac{6}{13}$ (g) $\frac{4}{7} \bigcirc \frac{4}{9}$ (h) $\frac{8}{19} \bigcirc \frac{8}{11}$

2. **Compare using > , <, or = .**

   (a) $\frac{3}{4} \bigcirc \frac{1}{5}$ (b) $\frac{7}{8} \bigcirc \frac{2}{3}$ (c) $\frac{3}{4} \bigcirc \frac{2}{3}$ (d) $\frac{1}{12} \bigcirc \frac{5}{7}$

   (e) $\frac{7}{10} \bigcirc \frac{3}{4}$ (f) $\frac{9}{10} \bigcirc \frac{7}{8}$ (g) $\frac{2}{8} \bigcirc \frac{3}{5}$ (h) $\frac{4}{5} \bigcirc \frac{3}{4}$

3. **Rearrange in ascending order.**

   (a) $\frac{9}{10}, \frac{9}{15}, \frac{9}{21}, \frac{9}{16}, \frac{9}{19}$ (b) $\frac{3}{15}, \frac{14}{15}, \frac{12}{15}, \frac{1}{15}, \frac{6}{15}$

   (c) $\frac{7}{8}, \frac{1}{6}, \frac{3}{4}, \frac{2}{3}$ (d) $\frac{3}{12}, \frac{7}{8}, \frac{2}{4}, \frac{2}{6}$

   (e) $\frac{1}{2}, \frac{2}{3}, \frac{3}{4}, \frac{1}{3}$ (f) $\frac{4}{5}, \frac{2}{3}, \frac{1}{2}, \frac{5}{6}, \frac{6}{10}$

4. **Rearrange in descending order.**

   (a) $\frac{10}{14}, \frac{10}{20}, \frac{10}{15}, \frac{10}{35}, \frac{10}{22}$ (b) $\frac{11}{19}, \frac{9}{19}, \frac{10}{19}, \frac{8}{19}, \frac{15}{19}$

   (c) $\frac{2}{3}, \frac{1}{5}, \frac{1}{2}, \frac{5}{6}$ (d) $\frac{1}{8}, \frac{5}{12}, \frac{2}{6}, \frac{3}{4}$

   (e) $\frac{2}{3}, \frac{3}{5}, \frac{5}{6}, \frac{3}{4}$ (f) $\frac{3}{4}, \frac{2}{3}, \frac{5}{8}, \frac{7}{9}, \frac{11}{12}$

Challenge

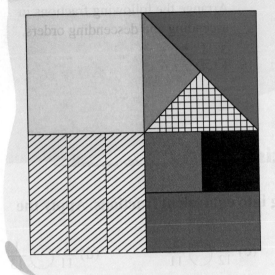

What fraction of the square are these?
Some are done for you.

  $\dfrac{1}{4}$

 $\dfrac{3}{12}$ or $\dfrac{1}{4}$

Addition

Adding Unlike Fractions

(a) Bholu, the farmer, planted rice on $\dfrac{1}{2}$ of his farm and corn

on $\dfrac{1}{4}$ of it. What fraction of the farm has rice and corn?

$$\dfrac{1}{2} + \dfrac{1}{4} = ?$$

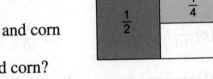

A fraction of
uneven parts
cannot be named!

**To add unlike fraction we must
first change them to like fractions**

- Find the equivalent fraction of $\dfrac{1}{2}$.

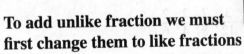

$$\dfrac{1 \, (\times 2)}{2 \, (\times 2)} = \dfrac{2}{4}$$

- Add the like fractions.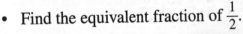

$$\dfrac{2}{4} + \dfrac{1}{4} = \dfrac{3}{4}$$

- $\dfrac{3}{4}$ of the farm is planted

with corn and rice.

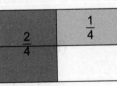 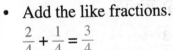 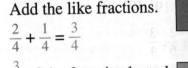 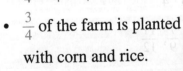 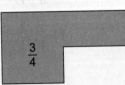 

(b) $\frac{2}{5} + \frac{1}{4} = ?$

or

LCM of 5 and 4 = 20

$\frac{2}{5} = \frac{4}{10} = \frac{6}{15} = \frac{8}{20}$ $\frac{1}{4} = \frac{2}{8} = \frac{3}{12} = \frac{4}{16} = \frac{5}{20}$

$\frac{2 \times 4}{5 \times 4} = \frac{8}{20}, \quad \frac{1 \times 5}{4 \times 5} = \frac{5}{20},$

$\frac{8}{20}$ and $\frac{5}{20}$ are like fractions

$\therefore \quad \frac{8}{20} + \frac{5}{20} = \frac{13}{20}$

$\frac{8}{20} + \frac{5}{20} = \frac{13}{20}$

> To find equivalent fractions with a common denominator, we can first find the LCM of the denominators.

Answer: $\frac{2}{5} + \frac{1}{4} = \frac{13}{20}$

(a) $\frac{1}{6} + \frac{3}{4} = ?$

LCM of 6 and 4 is 12.

$\frac{1}{6} = \frac{2}{12}$ ($6 \times 2 = 12$, so multiply both the numerator and the denominator by 2)

$\frac{3}{4} = \frac{9}{12}$ ($4 \times 3 = 12$, so multiply both the numerator and the denominator by 3)

$\frac{2}{12} + \frac{9}{12} = \frac{11}{12}$

> If the sum of two or more fractions is not in its lowest term, reduce it to the lowest term.

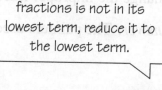

Answer: $\frac{1}{6} + \frac{3}{4} = \frac{11}{12}$

(b) Uday walked $\frac{2}{5}$ of a km and jogged $\frac{1}{10}$ of a km. How far did he go?

$\frac{2}{5} + \frac{1}{10} = ?$

LCM of 5 and 10 is 10.

$\frac{2 \times 2}{5 \times 2} = \frac{4}{10}$

$\frac{1}{10} = \frac{1}{10}$

$\frac{4}{10} + \frac{1}{10} = \frac{5}{10}$

$\frac{5}{10} = \frac{1}{2}$ (lowest term)

Answer: Uday went $\frac{1}{2}$ km.

If the sum of two or more fractions is an improper fraction, change the improper fraction to a mixed number.

(a) Vineeta walked $\frac{3}{4}$ of a km and jogged $\frac{2}{3}$ of a km. How far did she go?

$$\frac{3}{4} + \frac{2}{3} = ?$$

$$\frac{9}{12} + \frac{8}{12} = \frac{17}{12} = 1\frac{5}{12}$$

Answer: Vineeta went $1\frac{5}{12}$ km.

Adding Mixed Numbers

The painters used $3\frac{1}{2}$ ℓ of white paint and $2\frac{1}{4}$ ℓ of blue paint. How much paint did they use in all?

To add mixed numbers, change them to improper fractions first.

$$3\frac{1}{2} + 2\frac{1}{4} = ?$$

Change to **improper fractions**. $\longrightarrow \frac{7}{2} + \frac{9}{4}$

Change to **equivalent fractions** using the LCM method. $\longrightarrow \frac{14}{4} + \frac{9}{4} = \frac{23}{4}$

Change the improper fraction to a **mixed number**. $\longrightarrow \frac{23}{4} + 5\frac{3}{4}$

Answer: The painters used $5\frac{3}{4}$ ℓ of paint.

Exercise 4.4

1. **Add.**

   (a) $\frac{2}{3} + \frac{2}{9}$　　(b) $\frac{2}{7} + \frac{3}{4}$　　(c) $\frac{1}{7} + \frac{4}{5}$　　(d) $\frac{5}{6} + \frac{2}{3}$　　(e) $\frac{3}{4} + \frac{4}{5}$

   (f) $\frac{3}{7} + \frac{5}{6}$　　(g) $\frac{3}{8} + \frac{5}{16}$　　(h) $\frac{3}{8} + \frac{1}{4}$　　(i) $\frac{1}{2} + \frac{3}{4}$　　(j) $\frac{9}{16} + \frac{3}{8}$

   (k) $1\frac{3}{8} + \frac{2}{7}$　　(l) $2\frac{6}{7} + \frac{5}{7}$　　(m) $1\frac{5}{7} + 1\frac{2}{5}$　　(n) $1\frac{3}{13} + 2\frac{6}{7}$　　(o) $1\frac{4}{5} + 3\frac{3}{7}$

   (p) $1\frac{1}{2} + 2\frac{1}{4}$　　(q) $1\frac{3}{4} + 3\frac{2}{3}$　　(r) $3 + 1\frac{2}{3}$　　(s) $4\frac{1}{2} + 2\frac{3}{4}$　　(t) $3\frac{3}{4} + 2\frac{3}{4}$

Subtracting Unlike Fractions

Subtracting Proper Fraction

(a) Aparna ate $\frac{1}{2}$ of a chocolate bar. Vishu ate $\frac{1}{3}$ of a chocolate bar. How much more did Aparna eat than Vishu?

$\frac{1}{2} - \frac{1}{3} = ?$

To subtract unlike fractions, change them to equivalent fractions first.

$\frac{1}{2} = \frac{2}{4} = \frac{3}{6}$

$\frac{1}{3} = \frac{2}{6}$

$\frac{3}{6} - \frac{2}{6} = \frac{1}{6}.$

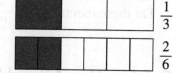

Answer: Aparna ate $\frac{1}{6}$ of a chocolate bar more than Vishu.

You can also use the LCM method to find the equivalent denominator.

(b) $\frac{5}{6} - \frac{3}{5} = ?$

LCM of 6 and 5 is 30.

$\frac{5 \times 5}{6 \times 5} = \frac{25}{30}$

$\frac{3 \times 6}{5 \times 6} = \frac{18}{30}$　　　$\frac{25}{30} - \frac{18}{30} = \frac{7}{30}$

Answer: $\frac{5}{6} - \frac{3}{5} = \frac{7}{30}$

If the difference is not in its lowest term, reduce the fraction to the lowest term.

(c) $\frac{5}{6} - \frac{1}{2} = ?$

$\frac{5}{6} - \frac{3}{6} = \frac{2}{6}$

$\frac{2}{6} = \frac{1}{3}$ (lowest terms)

Answer: $\frac{5}{6} - \frac{1}{2} = \frac{1}{3}$

Try This

(a) $\frac{3}{10} + \frac{1}{5}$

(b) $\frac{3}{4} - \frac{1}{2}$

Mental Maths

To solve $\frac{1}{8} + \frac{3}{4}$ To solve $\frac{1}{3} - \frac{3}{12}$

Think $\frac{3}{4} = \frac{6}{8}$ Think $\frac{1}{3} = \frac{4}{12}$

Then, $\frac{1}{8} + \frac{6}{8} = \frac{7}{8}$ So, $\frac{4}{12} - \frac{3}{12} = \frac{1}{12}$

Do these mentally: (a) $\frac{3}{10} + \frac{1}{5} = ?$ (b) $\frac{3}{4} - \frac{1}{2} = ?$

Subtracting Mixed Numbers

(a) The milkman had $2\frac{2}{3}$ litres of milk in the can. He sold $1\frac{1}{4}$ ℓ to a customer. How much is left in the can?

$2\frac{2}{3} - 1\frac{1}{4} = ?$

To subtract mixed numbers, change them to improper fractions first.

- Change to **improper fractions**. ⟶ $\frac{8}{3} - \frac{5}{4}$

- Change to **equivalent fractions**. ⟶ $\frac{32}{12} - \frac{15}{12} = \frac{17}{12}$

- Change the difference obtained to a **mixed number**. ⟶ $\frac{17}{12} = 1\frac{5}{12}$

Answer: There is $1\frac{5}{12}$ ℓ milk left in the can.

(b) $7 - 1\frac{3}{6} = ?$

$7 - 1\frac{3}{6} = \frac{7}{1} - \frac{9}{6} = \frac{42}{6} - \frac{9}{6} = \frac{33}{6} = \frac{11}{2} = 5\frac{1}{2}$

> Before you change an improper fraction to a mixed number in the answer first change it to its lowest terms.

Mental Maths

Since 1 is the same as $\frac{1}{1}, \frac{2}{2}, \frac{3}{3}, \frac{4}{4}$, etc., 5 is the same as $4\frac{2}{2}, 4\frac{3}{3}, 4\frac{4}{4}$, etc.

To solve mentally $5 - \frac{3}{4}$ Think: $4\frac{4}{4} - \frac{3}{4} = 4\frac{1}{4}$

To solve mentally $6 - 1\frac{2}{7}$ Think: $5\frac{7}{7} - 1\frac{2}{7} = 4\frac{5}{7}$

Do these mentally (a) $3 - \frac{1}{2}$ (b) $4 - 2\frac{1}{3}$

Exercise 4.5

1. Solve.

(a) $\frac{3}{4} - \frac{1}{2}$

(b) $\frac{7}{6} - \frac{3}{4}$

(c) $\frac{1}{4} - \frac{1}{6}$

(d) $\frac{2}{3} - \frac{1}{6}$

(e) $\frac{5}{6} - \frac{2}{3}$

(f) $\frac{7}{9} - \frac{1}{3}$

(g) $\frac{7}{10} - \frac{1}{2}$

(h) $\frac{5}{8} - \frac{0}{2}$

(i) $4\frac{2}{5} - 3\frac{1}{2}$

(j) $3\frac{4}{7} - 1\frac{4}{5}$

(k) $7 - 4\frac{1}{3}$

(l) $4\frac{3}{4} - \frac{1}{2}$

(m) $5\frac{2}{3} - 3$

(n) $8 - \frac{2}{3}$

(o) $6\frac{1}{3} - 2\frac{1}{4}$

(p) $11\frac{3}{7} - \frac{9}{16}$

Problem Solving

Decide whether to add or subtract.

(a) Vedika spent $\frac{1}{2}$ of her pocket money on a movie and $\frac{1}{4}$ on a new pen. What fraction of her allowance did she spend?

(b) Ankana did $\frac{3}{8}$ of her homework on Saturday and $\frac{1}{4}$ of the homework on Sunday. How much of the homework did she do over the weekend?

(c) Mrs Kumar bought 3 litres of milk in the morning. There was $\frac{5}{8}$ litres left in the evening. How much was used during the day?

(d) If $3\frac{2}{3}$ metres is cut from a ribbon which is $5\frac{1}{2}$ metres long, how much ribbon is left?

(e) A recipe needs $\frac{2}{5}$ cup of milk and $\frac{1}{3}$ cup of cream. How much more milk than cream is required?

(f) Sunita walked $\frac{1}{2}$ kilometre and jogged $\frac{7}{8}$ of a kilometre. How far did she go in all?

(g) Anamika gave $\frac{1}{8}$ of her stamp collection to her sister and $\frac{2}{7}$ to her friend. What fraction of her collection did she give away?

(h)  Akshay took $\frac{3}{4}$ of an hour to paint a picture. Rishi finished his painting in $\frac{1}{3}$ of an hour. How much longer did Akshay take?

Multiplication of Fractions

Multiplying Fractions and Whole Numbers

(a) Eight families went on a picnic. Each family had carried a cake for the picnic. $\frac{3}{4}$ of each cake was eaten.

We want to find out how much cake was eaten in all. We could find out using **repeated addition**.

$$\frac{3}{4} + \frac{3}{4} + \frac{3}{4} + \frac{3}{4} + \frac{3}{4} + \frac{3}{4} + \frac{3}{4} + \frac{3}{4} = \frac{24}{4} = 6$$

Or we could multiply

$8 \times \frac{3}{4} = ?$

To multiply a whole number and a fraction,

Step 1: Write the **whole number as a fraction.** ⟶ $\frac{8}{1} \times \frac{3}{4}$

Step 2: (a) **Multiply** the numerators. ⟶ $\frac{8}{1} \times \frac{3}{4} = \frac{24}{4}$
   (b) **Multiply** the denominators. ⟶

Step 3: **Simplify.** ⟶ $\frac{24}{4} = \frac{6}{1} = 6$

Answer: Six cakes were eaten at the picnic.

(b) $\frac{5}{7} \times 0 = ?$ (c) $\frac{6}{7} \times 1 = ?$

$\frac{5}{7} \times 0$ $\frac{6}{7} \times 1$

$$= \frac{5}{7} \times \frac{0}{1} = \frac{5 \times 0}{7 \times 1}$$

$$= \frac{0}{7}$$

$$= 0$$

Answer: $\frac{5}{7} \times 0 = 0$

$$= \frac{6}{7} \times \frac{1}{1} = \frac{6 \times 1}{7 \times 1}$$

$$= \frac{6}{7}$$

Answer: $\frac{6}{7} \times 1 = \frac{6}{7}$

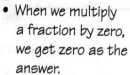
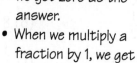

- When we multiply a fraction by zero, we get zero as the answer.
- When we multiply a fraction by 1, we get the same fraction.

Multiplying Fractions by Fractions

Pradeep's mother had made halwa and put it into a rectangular dish.

This is the amount of halwa that Pradeep saw was left in the dish.

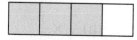 $\frac{3}{4}$ of the halwa was in the dish.

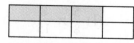 Pradeep ate $\frac{1}{2}$ of what was left.

How much did Pradeep eat?

To find $\frac{1}{2}$ of $\frac{3}{4}$ we could also **multiply**.

$\frac{1}{2}$ of $\frac{3}{4}$ is the same as $\frac{1}{2} \times \frac{3}{4}$.

$$\frac{1}{2} \times \frac{3}{4} = ?$$

To multiply a fraction by a fraction,

Step 1: **Multiply** the numerators.
Multiply the denominators.

$\longrightarrow$ $\frac{1 \times 3}{2 \times 4} = \frac{3}{8}$

Step 2: **Simplify** if possible. The fraction $\frac{3}{8}$ is already in the lowest form.

Answer: Pradeep ate $\frac{3}{8}$ of the halwa.

Use a Shortcut!

Sometimes it is possible to use a shortcut and **simplify before the last step.**

$$\frac{4}{5} \times \frac{7}{8}$$

$$= \frac{\overset{1}{\cancel{4}} \times 7}{5 \times \underset{2}{\cancel{8}}} = \frac{7}{10}$$

Look for common factors between the numerator and denominator and then divide. Here 4 divides both 4 and 8.

Refer Maths Lab Activity on Page 79

1. **Multiply. Give the answers in the lowest terms.**

   (a) $7 \times \dfrac{1}{2}$ (b) $8 \times \dfrac{4}{5}$ (c) $\dfrac{2}{7} \times 14$ (d) $5 \times \dfrac{2}{3}$

   (e) $\dfrac{1}{20} \times 20$ (f) $\dfrac{3}{7} \times 0$ (g) $18 \times \dfrac{2}{3}$ (h) $\dfrac{3}{4} \times 32$

   (i) $\dfrac{5}{12} \times 5$ (j) $\dfrac{8}{17} \times 1$ (k) $9 \times \dfrac{5}{6}$ (l) $4 \times \dfrac{1}{8}$

   (m) $0 \times \dfrac{7}{12}$ (n) $1 \times \dfrac{3}{5}$ (o) $\dfrac{4}{5} \times 10$

2. **Multiply. Use the shortcut where possible.**

   (a) $\dfrac{1}{2} \times \dfrac{3}{4}$ (b) $\dfrac{2}{3} \times \dfrac{4}{5}$ (c) $\dfrac{3}{2} \times \dfrac{1}{4}$ (d) $\dfrac{5}{3} \times \dfrac{7}{4}$

   (e) $\dfrac{4}{3} \times \dfrac{4}{5}$ (f) $\dfrac{2}{5} \times \dfrac{2}{7}$ (g) $\dfrac{1}{2} \times \dfrac{1}{2}$ (h) $\dfrac{2}{5} \times \dfrac{1}{3}$

   (i) $\dfrac{5}{12} \times \dfrac{7}{10}$ (j) $\dfrac{1}{6} \times \dfrac{9}{4}$ (k) $\dfrac{5}{33} \times \dfrac{1}{2}$ (l) $\dfrac{5}{8} \times \dfrac{8}{15}$

   (m) $\dfrac{6}{11} \times \dfrac{55}{42}$ (n) $\dfrac{7}{6} \times \dfrac{6}{21}$ (o) $\dfrac{3}{4} \times \dfrac{4}{3}$ (p) $\dfrac{2}{3} \times \dfrac{9}{14}$

Dividing Fractions and Whole Numbers

Multiplicative Inverse

To divide a whole number by a fraction we should know the meaning of **multiplicative inverse.**

Two numbers are the multiplicative inverse (M.I.) of each other when their product is 1.

Multiplicative inverse of $\dfrac{2}{3}$ is $\dfrac{3}{2}$ because

$$\dfrac{2}{3} \times \dfrac{3}{2} = \dfrac{6}{6} = 1.$$

Dividing a Whole Number by a Fraction

Mrs Abraham has made 2 kg of apple jam. She is putting it into separate bottles of $\dfrac{1}{4}$ kg each. How many bottles will She need?

1 kg   1 kg

The picture tells you that she will need 8 bottles. How will you find out the answer without the help of a picture?

$$2 \div \frac{1}{4} = ?$$

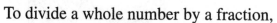

When we want to divide 2 by $\frac{1}{4}$, we write $2 \div \frac{1}{4}$, and we think 'how many $\frac{1}{4}$ in 2?'

To divide a whole number by a fraction,

Step 1: Write the **whole number as a fraction**. $\longrightarrow$ 　　　$\frac{2}{1}$ 　　$\div$ 　　$\frac{1}{4}$

　　　　　　　　　　　　　　　　　　　　　　　Dividend 　　**Divisor**

Step 2: Find the **multiplicative inverse** (M.I.) of the divisor. $\longrightarrow$ M.I. of $\frac{1}{4}$ is $\frac{4}{1}$

Step 3: **Multiply** the dividend and the M.I. of the divisor. $\longrightarrow \frac{2}{1} \times \frac{4}{1} = \frac{8}{1}$

Step 4: Write in **lowest terms.** $\longrightarrow$ 8 is in its lowest terms.

$$2 \div \frac{1}{4} = 8$$

Answer: Mrs Abraham will need 8 bottles of $\frac{1}{4}$ kg each.

Dividing a Fraction by a whole Number

$\frac{3}{4}$ bottle of orange juice has to be poured into 9 glasses. If an equal amount of juice has to be put into each glass, how much of the juice will each glass hold.?

$$\frac{3}{4} \div 9 = ?$$

To divide a fraction by a whole number,

Step 1: Write the **whole number as a fraction.** $\longrightarrow$ 　　　$\frac{3}{4}$ 　$\div$ 　$\frac{9}{1}$

　　　　　　　　　　　　　　　　　　　　　　　Dividend 　　**Divisor**

Step 2: Find the **M.I. of the divisor**. $\longrightarrow$ M.I. of $\frac{9}{1}$ is $\frac{1}{9}$.

Step 3: **Multiply** the dividend and the M.I. of the divisor. $\longrightarrow \frac{3}{4} \times \frac{1}{9} = \frac{3}{36}$

Step 4: **Simplify.** $\longrightarrow \frac{3}{36} = \frac{1}{12}$

Answer: Each glass will hold $\frac{1}{12}$ of the juice in the bottle.

Dividing Fractions by Fractions

Shristi has a piece of lace $\frac{8}{9}$ of a metre long. She wants to cut it into pieces that are $\frac{1}{9}$ of a metre long. How many pieces will she get?

Think: How many ninths in $\frac{8}{9}$?

$$\frac{8}{9} \div \frac{1}{9} = ?$$

To divide a fraction by a fraction,

Step 1: Find the **M.I. of the divisor.** $\longrightarrow$ M.I. of $\frac{1}{9}$ is $\frac{9}{1}$.

Step 2: **Multiply** the dividend and the M.I. of the divisor. $\longrightarrow \frac{8}{9} \times \frac{9}{1} = \frac{72}{9}$

Step 3: **Simplify.** $\longrightarrow \frac{72}{9} = \frac{8}{1} = 8$

Answer: Shristi will get 8 pieces of lace.

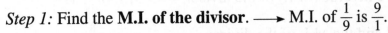

Exercise 4.7

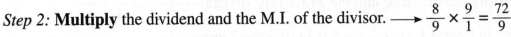

1. Divide.

(a) $\frac{1}{2} \div \frac{7}{12}$ (b) $\frac{5}{9} \div \frac{2}{3}$ (c) $\frac{1}{3} \div \frac{5}{8}$ (d) $0 \div \frac{3}{8}$ (e) $\frac{3}{8} \div \frac{3}{5}$

(f) $\frac{6}{7} \div \frac{1}{3}$ (g) $\frac{1}{3} \div \frac{1}{3}$ (h) $\frac{3}{5} \div \frac{1}{5}$ (i) $\frac{4}{7} \div \frac{3}{4}$ (j) $\frac{3}{4} \div \frac{4}{5}$

(k) $0 \div \frac{3}{5}$ (l) $\frac{2}{3} \div \frac{1}{6}$ (m) $\frac{4}{5} \div \frac{1}{4}$ (n) $\frac{7}{8} \div \frac{3}{4}$ (o) $\frac{1}{2} \div \frac{2}{3}$

(p) $\frac{3}{4} \div \frac{3}{4}$ (q) $\frac{2}{7} \div \frac{1}{4}$ (r) $\frac{2}{7} \div \frac{2}{3}$ (s) $\frac{3}{5} \div \frac{1}{2}$ (t) $\frac{2}{3} \div \frac{1}{4}$

2. Solve.

(a) $3 \div \frac{1}{5}$ (b) $7 \div \frac{1}{3}$ (c) $8 \div \frac{1}{6}$ (d) $1 \div \frac{1}{10}$ (e) $6 \div \frac{3}{4}$

(f) $\frac{9}{7} \div 3$ (g) $\frac{2}{5} \div 2$ (h) $\frac{1}{2} \div 7$ (i) $\frac{1}{3} \div 12$ (j) $\frac{1}{20} \div 3$

(k) $2 \div \frac{2}{3}$ (l) $5 \div \frac{2}{5}$ (m) $\frac{6}{7} \div 5$ (n) $\frac{3}{8} \div 8$ (o) $6 \div \frac{2}{3}$

(p) $14 \div \frac{3}{7}$ (q) $\frac{4}{5} \div 11$ (r) $\frac{3}{7} \div 22$ (s) $\frac{4}{5} \div 10$ (t) $15 \div \frac{7}{8}$

3. Solve using multiplication or division.

(a) A painter uses $\frac{3}{5}$ of a can of paint to cover one wall of a house. How many cans of paint will he need to cover 7 such walls?

(b) Nandita used $\frac{1}{4}$ of a sheet of clear plastic to cover her book. How many sheets would she need to cover 12 books?

(c)  Three children are sharing $\frac{2}{3}$ of a pizza. What fraction of the pizza will each child get?

(d) Kiran is giving away $\frac{1}{4}$ of his bookmark collection to 5 of his friends. If each friend gets the same number of bookmarks, what fraction of the collection has each child received?

(e) A packet of soup makes 9 bowls of servings. How many $\frac{3}{4}$ bowls of servings are possible?

(f) Mrs Ghosh bought 1 kg of grapes and served each member of her family an equal amount. How many people did she serve it to if each person got $\frac{1}{4}$ of a kg?

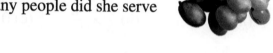

Challenge

Rahul's mother baked seven pastries. He gave half of what she made plus half a pastry to his friend Nina. He then gave half of what was left plus half a pastry to another friend, Rohit. Then he kept half of what was left plus a pastry for himself. How many pastries did each person get?

Project

Find a recipe for fruit salad that serves 4 people. Use cup and spoon measurements. Make the fruit salad. Rewrite the recipe for 8 people. Rewrite the recipe for 2 people.

CHAPTER CHECK-UP

1. **Find two equivalent fractions for each of the following.**

    (a) $\frac{4}{5}$ (b) $\frac{7}{9}$ (c) $\frac{6}{11}$

2. **Reduce to the lowest terms.**

    (a) $\frac{16}{24}$ (b) $\frac{32}{48}$ (c) $\frac{81}{90}$

3. **Compare using < or >.**

    (a) $\frac{1}{7} \bigcirc \frac{1}{3}$ (b) $\frac{2}{9} \bigcirc \frac{5}{9}$ (c) $\frac{3}{5} \bigcirc \frac{2}{7}$ (d) $\frac{6}{9} \bigcirc \frac{2}{5}$

4. **Solve.**

    (a) $\frac{3}{13} + \frac{7}{13}$ (b) $\frac{2}{4} + \frac{5}{5}$ (c) $\frac{8}{9} + \frac{2}{9} + \frac{3}{9}$ (d) $\frac{2}{7} + \frac{3}{5}$

    (e) $\frac{4}{5} + \frac{8}{9} + \frac{2}{3}$ (f) $\frac{7}{17} - \frac{4}{17}$ (g) $\frac{7}{9} - \frac{7}{12}$ (h) $3\frac{2}{5} - 2\frac{1}{10}$

5. **Solve.**

    (a) $\frac{5}{7} \times 2$ (b) $\frac{7}{3} \times \frac{4}{11}$ (c) $0 \times \frac{7}{13}$ (d) $\frac{3}{6} \times \frac{4}{12}$ (e) $\frac{2}{11} \times \frac{5}{6}$

    (f) $\frac{2}{7} \div \frac{3}{4}$ (g) $\frac{4}{7} \div 5$ (h) $\frac{4}{5} \div \frac{1}{2}$ (i) $16 \div \frac{3}{4}$ (j) $\frac{5}{11} \div \frac{3}{7}$

6. (a) Zeenat bought 5 kg of wax to make some decorative candles. If she needs $\frac{1}{10}$ kg per candle, how many candles can she make?

(b)

Divya spent $2\frac{1}{2}$ hours watching birds on Saturday and $1\frac{3}{4}$ hours watching birds on Sunday. How many hours over the weekend did Divya spent on bird watching?

(c) Prateek studied for $6\frac{1}{3}$ hours in one week and $4\frac{3}{4}$ hours the next. How much longer did he study in the first week?

MATHS LAB ACTIVITY

Multiplication of Fractions

Objective: To build an understanding of multiplication of fractions.
Materials Required: Square-lined paper, crayons of two colours.
Preparation: Students work independently or in pairs.

Steps:

To solve $\frac{1}{3} \times \frac{2}{5}$

1. Since the two denominators are 3 and 5, the students draw a rectangle of sides 3 squares by 5 squares on the square-lined paper.

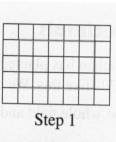

Step 1

2. Then one student colours $\frac{1}{3}$ of the rectangle with blue horizontal lines.

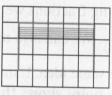

Step 2

3. The second student colours $\frac{2}{5}$ of the rectangle with red vertical lines.
   What fraction of the sheet does have both vertical and horizontal lines?

   This shows that $\frac{1}{3} \times \frac{2}{5} = \frac{2}{15}$

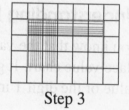

Step 3

Try this out:

  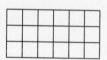

$\frac{1}{2} \times \frac{3}{4} = \boxed{}$ $\frac{2}{5} \times \frac{1}{4} = \boxed{}$ $\frac{4}{6} \times \frac{1}{3} = \boxed{}$ $\frac{2}{3} \times \frac{3}{4} = \boxed{}$

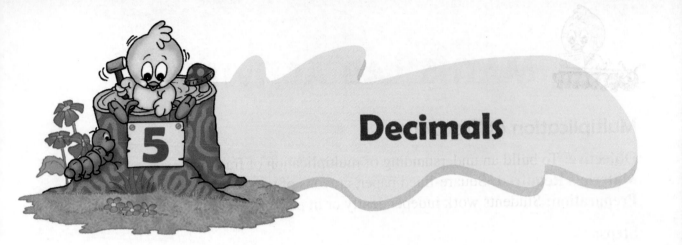

Decimals

Decimals

Kannan has planted potatoes in two of his fields like this. We can say he has planted one whole field and $\frac{3}{10}$ of another.

Using fractions we would write this as $1\frac{3}{10}$. We can also use **decimals** to convey

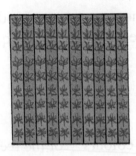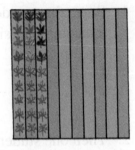

the same idea. Using decimals we would write this as 1.3. **The digits to the right of the point shows that it is less than one whole.**

Understanding Decimals

You know that the value of a digit decreases every time it moves to the right in the place value chart. It gets ten times smaller for every move to the right. Watch the place value of the digit 1 in this chart.

H T O	Value of 1	
1 5 2	100	
1 6	10	(100 ÷ 10)
1	1	(10 ÷ 10)

Tenths

What happens when the digit moves further to the right?

H T O . tenths	Value of digit	
0 . 1	$\frac{1}{10}$	(1 ÷ 10)

0.1 is read as one tenth.

1 is further divided into 10 equal parts and each part is called a tenth.

The fractional form of one tenth is $\frac{1}{10}$.

The decimal form of one tenth is 0.1.

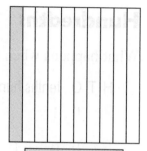

1 one = 10 tenths

Whole numbers and decimal numbers are combined like this:

0.1 = 1 tenth

Whole number part ⟵ **2.4** ⟶ **Decimal part**

↓

Decimal point

Where there is no whole number, remember to write 'O' in the whole number position before the decimal.

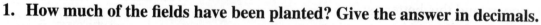

Exercise 5.1

1. How much of the fields have been planted? Give the answer in decimals.

(a)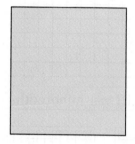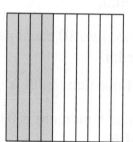

(b)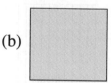

(c)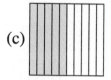

(d)

(Note: additional field figures for rows (a)–(d) 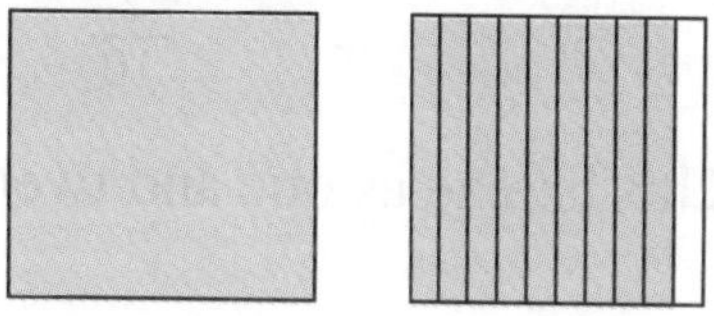 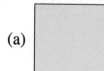   )

2. Match the following.

(a) 4.1   (i) Two and three tenths
(b) 2.3   (ii) One and one tenth
(c) 1.1   (iii) Five tenths
(d) 0.5   (iv) Four and one tenth

Hundredths

What happens when the digit moves still further to the right?

H T O . tenths hundredths	Value of digit	
0 . 1	$\frac{1}{10}$	$(1 \div 10)$
0 . 0 1	$\frac{1}{100}$	$(\frac{1}{10} \div 10)$

0.01 is read as one hundredth.

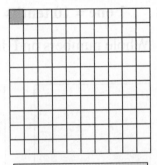

0.01 = 1 hundredth

- 1 tenth is further divided into 10 equal parts and each part is called 1 hundredth.

- The fractional form of one hundredth is $\frac{1}{100}$.

- The decimal form of one hundredth is 0.01.
  1 tenth = 10 hundredths

Kannan has pasted Indian stamps in his album like this.

He has used 1.07 pages for his Indian stamps.

$1 \qquad + \qquad \frac{7}{100} = 1.07$

After a few months he got 20 more stamps and now the pages look like this.

He now needs 1.27 pages for his Indian stamps.

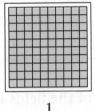
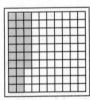

$1 \qquad + \qquad \frac{27}{100} = 1.27$

We can understand this better as:

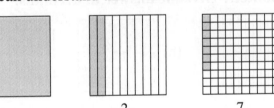
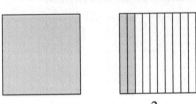

$$1 \qquad + \qquad \frac{2}{10} \qquad + \qquad \frac{7}{100} \qquad = 1 + \frac{27}{100} = 1.27$$

This is read as one and twenty-seven hundredths.

Thousandths

- 1 hundredth is further divided into 10 equal parts. Each part is called 1 thousandth.

- The fractional form of one thousandth is $\frac{1}{1000}$.

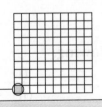
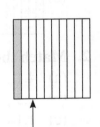

0.001 = 1 thousandth

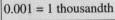

The corner box has been shown bigger here. All other boxes, if enlarged, would look like this.

- The decimal form of one thousandth is 0.001.

1 hundredth = 10 thousandths

Ones	tenths	hundredths	thousandths
3	8	1	6

$= 3.816 = \frac{3816}{1000}$

This is read as **three and eight hundred sixteen thousandths.**

Exercise 5.2

1. Match the following:

(a)

0.26

(b)

2.08

(c)

1.43

(d)

3.2

2. For the number 186.452 write the digit in the:

(a) tens place (b) tenths place

(c) hundreds place (d) hundredths place

(e) ones place (f) thousandths place

3. Build a decimal with:

(a) 7 in the tenths place, 4 in the ones place.

(b) 9 in the tenths place, 6 in the hundredths place, 8 in the ones place, 5 in the tens place.

(c) 5 in the ones place, 7 in the tenths place, 8 in the hundredths place, 3 in the thousandths place.

4. Give the next three numbers.

(a) 1.2, 1.3, 1.4 _____

(b) 5.92, 5.93, 5.94 _____

(c) 11.8, 11.9, 12.0 _____

(d) 8.001, 8.002, 8.003 _____

(e) 6.02, 6.03, 6.04 _____

(f) 4.23, 4.24, 4.25 _____

Converting Fractions to Decimals

Fractions with denominator 10, 100, 1000

$$\frac{3}{10} = 0.3 \qquad \frac{24}{10} = 2.4 \qquad \frac{153}{10} = 15.3 \qquad \frac{1608}{10} = 160.8$$

$$\frac{3}{100} = 0.03 \qquad \frac{24}{100} = 0.24 \qquad \frac{153}{100} = 1.53 \qquad \frac{1608}{100} = 16.08$$

$$\frac{3}{1000} = 0.003 \qquad \frac{24}{1000} = 0.024 \qquad \frac{153}{1000} = 0.153 \qquad \frac{1608}{1000} = 1.608$$

The zeros in the denominator tell you the number of decimal places.

Converting Decimals to Fractions

Reading a decimal correctly helps you to change it easily into fractions.

7 tenths	12 hundredths	1 and 4 thousandths

$$0.7 = \frac{7}{10} \qquad 0.12 = \frac{12}{100} \qquad 1.004 = 1\frac{4}{1000}$$

You may also use fractional expansion to convert it.

(a) $2.7 = 2 + \frac{7}{10}$

$$= \frac{2}{1} + \frac{7}{10} = \frac{2 \times 10}{1 \times 10} + \frac{7}{10} = \frac{20}{10} + \frac{7}{10} = \frac{27}{10}$$

Answer: $2.7 = \frac{27}{10} = 2\frac{7}{10}$

(b) $0.36 = \frac{3}{10} + \frac{6}{100}$

$$= \frac{3 \times 10}{10 \times 10} + \frac{6}{100} = \frac{30}{100} + \frac{6}{100} = \frac{36}{100}$$

Answer: $0.36 = \frac{36}{100}$

Try This

(a) Show $3\frac{4}{10}$ as a decimal.

(b) Express 3.06 as a fraction.

Use a shortcut!

(a) Express 3.02 as a fraction.

Step 1: **Count** the number of decimal places (two, in this example).   3.02

Step 2: Rewrite the **number without the decimal**. That is the numerator. →   302

Step 3: Write the **denominator** with as many zeros as decimal places. → $\dfrac{302}{100}$

Answer: $3.02 = \dfrac{302}{100}$

(b) Express 13.184 as a fraction

$13.184 \rightarrow 13184 \rightarrow \dfrac{13184}{1000}$

Answer: $13.184 = \dfrac{13184}{1000}$

Decimal and Fractional Expansion

Take the number 36.258

Decimal expansion of 36.258	$30 + 6 + 0.2 + 0.05 + 0.008 = 36.258$
Fraction expansion of 36.258	$30 + 6 + \dfrac{2}{10} + \dfrac{5}{100} + \dfrac{8}{1000} = 36\dfrac{258}{1000} = 36.258$

Exercise 5.3

1. **Write a decimal for each of the following:**
   (a) $6.0 + 0.7 + 0.09$ (b) $5 + 0.1 + 0.008$ (c) $3 + 0.08 + 0.005$
   (d) $0.8 + 0.06 + 0.007$ (e) $30 + 1 + 0.2 + 0.08$ (f) $10 + 7 + 0.5 + 0.02 + 0.001$

2. **Write a decimal for each of the following:**
   (a) $9 + \dfrac{6}{10} + \dfrac{8}{100} + \dfrac{3}{1000}$ (b) $1 + \dfrac{1}{10} + \dfrac{6}{1000}$ (c) $40 + 3 + \dfrac{7}{100} + \dfrac{5}{1000}$

   (d) $50 + 6 + \dfrac{8}{1000}$ (e) $\dfrac{3}{10} + \dfrac{8}{100} + \dfrac{7}{1000}$ (f) $20 + \dfrac{9}{1000}$

3. **Give the decimal and fractional expansion of the following:**
   (a) 9.875   (b) 23.076   (c) 14.807   (d) 396.99   (e) 87.1

4. **Express as a decimal.**
   (a) $\dfrac{72}{100}$ (b) $\dfrac{8}{10}$ (c) $\dfrac{9}{100}$ (d) $\dfrac{137}{100}$
   (e) $\dfrac{186}{1000}$ (f) $\dfrac{4}{1000}$ (g) $\dfrac{1171}{1000}$ (h) $\dfrac{454}{10}$

(i) $\frac{42}{100}$ (j) $\frac{1876}{100}$ (k) $\frac{23}{100}$ (l) $\frac{9018}{10}$

5. Express as a fraction.
(a) 0.04   (b) 15.63   (c) 24.9   (d) 0.175
(e) 26.004   (f) 0.86   (g) 1.31   (h) 7.105

6. Express as a fraction and a decimal. One is done for you.

(a)

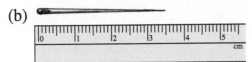

Length of the knife = $\frac{4}{10}$ m = 0.4 m

(b)

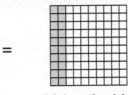

(c)

Equivalent Decimals

2 tenths	=	20 hundredths		200 thousandths
0.2	=	0.20		0.200

Each of the 100 boxes in the last grid are further divided into 10 boxes.

All three decimal numbers shown above have the same value and so they are called **equivalent decimals**.

This can also be checked by comparing the decimals with equivalent fractions:

$$\frac{2}{10} = \frac{20}{100} = \frac{200}{1000}$$

$$0.2 = 0.20 = 0.200$$

$$0.2 = 0.2 = 0.2$$

Writing or removing zeros at the end of a decimal number does not change its value.

Like and Unlike Decimals

Decimals with the same number of decimal places are called like decimals.

(a)   0.3   4.5   8.7   (*one decimal place each*)
(b) 12.17   1.04   263.11   (*two decimal places each*)
(c)   1.093   0.847   11.970   (*three decimal places each*)

Decimals having different number of decimal places are called unlike decimals.

(a)   0.7   2.81
(b)   18.24   13.8
(c)   0.724   8.74

Unlike decimals can also be equivalent decimals.

0.7, 0.70, 0.700 are *unlike but equivalent decimals.*

> These unlike decimals have been converted into like decimals by finding their equivalent decimals up to three decimal places.

Converting unlike decimals into like decimals

Unlike decimals can be converted to like decimals by finding their equivalent decimals.

Unlike decimals	1.7	8.36	9.755
	↓	↓	↓
Like decimals	1.700	8.360	9.755

 **Exercise 5.4**

1. **Fill in the blanks with equivalent decimals.**
   (a) 0.6 = 0.60 = _____   (b) 1.7 = 1.70 = _____   (c) 62.4 = 62.40 = _____
   (d) _____ = 0.80 = 0.800   (e) 2.4 = _____ = 2.400   (f) 87.5 = _____ = _____

2. **Convert these unlike decimals into like decimals.**
   (a) 9.5   9.15   (b) 13.5   1.72   0.845   (c) 1.75   3.9   8.084
   (d) 0.14   32.5   9.3   (e) 8.4   9.76   3.005   (f) 24.93   707.124

Comparing and Ordering Decimals

Comparing decimals

(a) Using mathematical models.

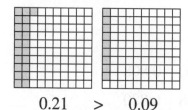   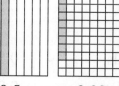   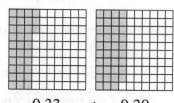

   0.21   >   0.09   0.5   >   0.08   0.33   <   0.39

(b) Trisha and Tanay were having a roller-skating race.
   Trisha finished in 50.08 seconds.

Tanay finished in 50.3 seconds.

Who won the race?

The child who took less time won the race. To find out which child took less time, we need to compare:

50.08 ◯ 50.3
          ↓   } Convert into like decimals.
50.08 ◯ 50.30

Now compare like you do for whole numbers.

5008 < 5030

50.08 < 50.30

Answer: Trisha won the race because 50.08 < 50.3.

To compare decimals, first convert them to like decimals.

Ordering decimals

(a) During a medical inspection, the weight of four children was recorded as shown. Rewrite the list in descending order (*place the heaviest child first*).

Naren   43.17 kg

Natasha   43.7 kg

Vidya   42.09 kg

Varun   41.8 kg

To put them in descending order, convert to like decimals of two places each.

Naren	Natasha	Vidya	Varun
43.17	43.7	42.09	41.8
↓	↓	↓	↓
43.17	43.70	42.09	41.80

Now rearrange as you would do for whole numbers.

(4370   4317   4209   4180)

Answer: Natasha   43.7 kg
            Naren   43.17 kg   } *placed in descending order*
            Vidya   42.09 kg
            Varun   41.8 kg

(b) Rewrite in ascending order.

0.88   0.8   0.808

Step 1: Convert to like decimals.   ⟶   0.880   0.800   0.808

Step 2: Write in ascending order.   ⟶   0.800   0.808   0.880

Answer: 0.8   0.808   0.88

Exercise 5.5

1. Colour to compare.

(a)
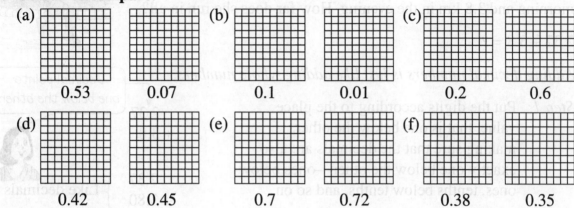
0.53   0.07

(b)
0.1   0.01

(c)
0.2   0.6

(d)
0.42   0.45

(e)
0.7   0.72

(f)
0.38   0.35

2. Compare using <, >, or =.

(a) 9.099 ◯ 9.99   (b) 70.08 ◯ 70.7   (c) 6.6 ◯ 6.066

(d) 96.550 ◯ 96.55   (e) 5.091 ◯ 5.09   (f) 0.5 ◯ 0.15

(g) 6.4 ◯ 6.359   (h) 0.3 ◯ 2.895   (i) 0.76 ◯ 0.8

3. Rewrite in descending order.

(a) 8.06   8.059   8.013   8.3   (d) 3.48   4.2   3.8   4.02

(b) 19.4   1.945   19.46   1.95   (e) 6.8   8.66   8.06   6.08

(c) 8.63   80.002   8.6   80.2   (d) 3.9   3.09   3.91   3.019

4. Rewrite in ascending order.

(a) 0.04   1.04   0.14   1.14   (b) 20   19.09   20.01   19.9

(c) 14.19   19.14   14.9   19.4   (d) 6.23   6.32   6.4   6

(e) 9.09   0.99   1.1   6   (f) 7.162   7.23   7.02   7.2

Challenge

Use the digits   [7] [8] [2]

🌸 Build the biggest number less than one.

🌸 Build the smallest number less than one.

🌸 The biggest number between 7 and 8.

Addition of Decimals

Alka is practising for her school sports day. She runs 2.37 km in the morning and 3.8 km in the evening. How far does she run in all?

2.37 + 3.8 = ?

Adding decimal numbers is just like adding whole numbers.

Step 1: Put the digits according to the place value, that is one below the other, making sure that the decimals are also exactly one below the other—ones below ones, tenths below tenths, and so on.

Step 2: Change the decimals to like decimals.

Step 3: Add as usual. Start from the hundredths. Carry over if needed.

Step 4: Place the decimal point in the answer in the same place as the numbers above it.

Answer: Alka practises running 6.17 km in all.

$$\begin{array}{r} 2.37 \\ + 3.8 \\ \hline \end{array}$$

Decimal points one below the other.

$$\left.\begin{array}{r} 2.37 \\ + 3.80 \\ \hline \end{array}\right\} \text{Like decimals}$$

$$\begin{array}{r} 2.37 \\ + 3.80 \\ \hline \end{array}$$

$$\begin{array}{r} 6.17 \\ \hline \end{array}$$

Do not forget the decimal point in the answer.

This is just like adding money!

Common Mistake!

$$\begin{array}{r} 5.4 \\ + 6.7 \\ \hline 121 \end{array} \text{✗} \qquad \begin{array}{r} 5.4 \\ + 6.7 \\ \hline 12.1 \end{array} \text{✓} \qquad \begin{array}{r} 14 \\ + 0.59 \\ \hline \end{array} \text{✗} \qquad \begin{array}{r} 14.00 \\ + 0.59 \\ \hline \end{array} \text{✓}$$

 **Exercise 5.6**

1. **Add.**
   (a) 23.11 + 3.8
   (b) 13.01 + 1.1 + 1.98
   (c) 9 + 1.8
   (d) 562.9 + 49.3
   (e) 0.1 + 1 + 11.40
   (f) 162.1 + 16.21
   (g) 9.85 + 0.61
   (h) 23 + 18.94
   (i) 17.01 + 18.1

2. **Compare using >, <, or =.**
   (a) 5.72 + 3.80 ◯ 8.52
   (b) 2.5 + 3.09 ◯ 5.95
   (c) 3 + 0.05 ◯ 0.35
   (d) 10 + 0.01 ◯ 10.01
   (e) 61.2 + 5.31 ◯ 48.72 + 12.9
   (f) 21.93 + 1.16 ◯ 1.8 + 20.16

3. Colour to show how much juice in all. One is done for you.

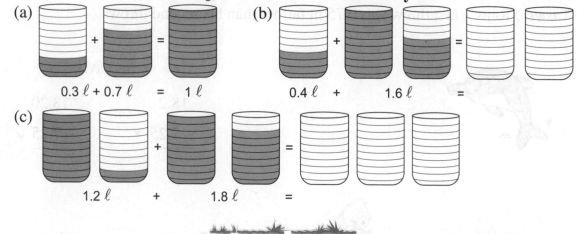

(a)

0.3 ℓ + 0.7 ℓ = 1 ℓ

(b)

0.4 ℓ + 1.6 ℓ =

(c)

1.2 ℓ + 1.8 ℓ =

Project

Make separate decimal cards using the numbers shown. Mix them up. Place them face down. Pick any two at a time. If they add up to 1 keep them. If they don't, put them back. Continue till you have found all the pairs.

0.1	0.5	0.9	0.85	0.35	0.55
0.2	0.6	0.25	0.45	0.65	
0.4	0.8	0.15	0.75	0.50	

Subtraction of Decimals

Rajeev was measuring how far he could throw a ball. On the first try, it went 17.5 m. On the second try, it went 16.75 m. How much farther did it go on the first try?

17.5 – 16.75 = ?

Subtracting decimal numbers is just like subtracting whole numbers.

Step 1: Put the greater number on top and the lesser one below, taking care to match the place value and keeping the decimals one below the other.

$$17.5 \\ -\ 16.75$$

Step 2: Convert them into like decimals.

$$\left.\begin{array}{r} 17.50 \\ -\ 16.75 \end{array}\right\} \text{Like decimals}$$

Step 3: Subtract as usual. Regroup if necessary.

$$\begin{array}{r} 17.50 \\ -\ 16.75 \\ \hline 0.75 \end{array}$$

Do not forget the decimal point in the answer.

The decimal point in the answer must be in the same place as in the numbers above it.
Answer: Rajiv's first throw was 0.75 m farther than his second throw.

Common Mistake!

18.2	18.20
− 7.25 ✗	− 7.25 ✓

Exercise 5.7

1. **Subtract.**
   (a) 9.32 – 4.16   (b) 18.43 – 9.26   (c) 7 – 4.32   (d) 9.4 – 3.13
   (e) 11.01 – 10.11   (f) 24.1 – 18.39   (g) 0.62 – 0.23   (h) 8 – 6.04
   (i) 14.1 – 9.25   (j) 4.37 – 0.65   (k) 12.35 – 4   (l) 15.1 – 12.05

2. What should be added to 2.1 to get 10?

3. What should be taken away from 15 to get 3.96?

4. **Play a game.**

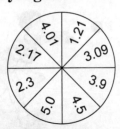

   • Draw a circle like this in your notebook.
   • Drop two paper clips or *rajma* seeds on the circle.
   • Subtract the smaller number from the greater one.
   • Ask a friend to do the same.
   • Whose difference is smaller?
   • Record all your work.

5. **The table below gives the names of the top runners of a 100 metre race. Study the table and answer the questions below.**

Names	100 m race timings
Rahul	19.52 seconds
Rohan	20.2 seconds
Ananth	20.5 seconds
Suraj	19.25 seconds
Prashant	20.05 seconds

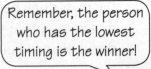

Remember, the person who has the lowest timing is the winner!

   (a) How much faster did the winner run than the person who was last?
   (b) How much slower did Prashant run than Rahul?

Problem Solving

Application in real life

1. The winning team got a score of 30 points. The team that came second got a score of 23.5 points. By how many points did the winning team win?

2.  Akshit's father drove 158.3 km on Monday and 79.8 km on Tuesday. How many kilometres less did he drive on Tuesday?

3. A bean plant measured 8.5 cm on Friday. It grew another 0.75 cm on Saturday. What was its height on Saturday?

4. The thickness of one book is 3.8 cm. The thickness of another is 2.03 cm. What is the thickness of the two books together when placed one on top of the other?

5. Smriti, Saroj, and Shamin were comparing their test marks. They got 15.05, 15.25, and 15.5 marks respectively. Who did the best?

6. In a quiz competition, team A secured 84.5 points and team B secured 85 points. Which team won the quiz?

7. Shanay can swim the 100 m lap in 68.1 seconds. Swapneel can swim the same distance in 68.02 seconds. Who is faster?

8. Pranay has a milometer on his motorcycle that shows how far he has travelled. It shows 62.5 km now. How much farther does he have to ride to reach 100 km?

Multiplication of Decimals

Multiplying by Whole Numbers

Prashant needs to buy 3 special pencils for his art exam. If each pencil costs Rs 5.25, how much will Prashant have to pay?

$5.25 + 5.25 + 5.25 = ?$

Or

$3 \times 5.25 = ?$

Step 1:	Multiply as with whole numbers ignoring the decimal.	5.25 × 3 ――― 1575
Step 2:	Count the number of decimal places in the factors.	5.25 (*2 decimal places*) × 3 (*0 decimal places*) ――― 1575
Step 3:	Show the number of decimal places in the product.	5.25 × 3 ――― 15.75 (*2 + 0 = 2 decimal places*)

Answer: Prashant has to pay Rs 15.75.

Remember

- The number of decimal places in the product equals the sum of the number of decimal places in the factors.
- While counting the digits in the product to place the decimal point, start from the right.

Exercise 5.8

1. Introduce the decimal point at the correct place in the product.

(a) 2.5 × 9 = 225 (b) 17 × 1.17 = 1989 (c) 0.04 × 8 = 32

(d) 3.81 × 6 = 2286 (e) 24 × 1.1 = 264 (f) 8 × 1.01 = 808

2. Multiply only the first in the series. Then use the rules of decimals to fill in the rest.

(a)
127	12.7	1.27
× 8	× 8	× 8

(b)
312	312	312
× 5	× 0.5	× 0.05

3. Multiply.

(a) 5.3 × 9 (b) 8.4 × 11 (c) 24 × 0.9 (d) 1.9 × 68

(e) 2 × 3.45 (f) 7 × 8.39 (g) 17.42 × 8 (h) 1.23 × 8

Mental Maths

To find 5.2×3

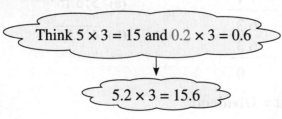

Think $5 \times 3 = 15$ and $0.2 \times 3 = 0.6$

$5.2 \times 3 = 15.6$

(a) 4.3×2 (e) 5.2×4
(b) 9.2×2 (f) 8.3×3
(c) 6.2×3 (g) 7.3×4
(d) 4.2×3 (h) 3.4×3

Division in Decimal Numbers

Dividing by Whole Numbers

(a) When paper is needed in large quantities, it can be bought in kilograms. Three friends bought 4.35 kg of paper. How did they share it among themselves?

$4.35 \div 3 = ?$

Dividing by decimals is just like dividing whole numbers, except for placing the decimal point.

$$3 \overline{)\ 4\ .\ 3\ 5}$$

Decimal point directly above the decimal in the dividend.

Step 1: Place the **decimal point in the quotient** directly above the decimal point.

Step 2: **Divide** as if you were dividing whole numbers.

Divide the ones	Divide the tenths	Divide the hundredths
$\begin{array}{r} 1\,. \\ 3\,\overline{)\,4\,.\,3\,5} \\ -3 \\ \hline 1 \end{array}$	$\begin{array}{r} 1\,.\,4 \\ 3\,\overline{)\,4\,.\,3\,5} \\ -3\downarrow \\ \hline 1\ 3 \\ -1\ 2 \\ \hline 1 \end{array}$	$\begin{array}{r} 1\,.\,4\,5 \\ 3\,\overline{)\,4\,.\,3\,5} \\ -3 \\ \hline 1\ 3 \\ -1\ 2 \\ \hline 1\ 5 \\ -1\ 5 \\ \hline 0 \end{array}$

Do not show the decimal in the working of the sum. It should appear only in the dividend and the quotient.

$4.35 \div 3 = 1.45$

Answer: Each friend gets 1.45 kg of paper.

(b) 1.33 ÷ 7 (*divisor greater than dividend*)

$$7\overline{)1.33}$$

$$\begin{array}{r} 0. \\ 7\overline{)1.33} \end{array}$$

$$\begin{array}{r} 0.19 \\ 7\overline{)1.33} \\ -7\downarrow \\ \hline 63 \\ -63 \\ \hline 0 \end{array}$$

Check: $\begin{array}{r} 0.19 \\ \times 7 \\ \hline 1.33 \end{array}$ **Divisor × Quotient = Dividend**

Remainders while Dividing Decimals

(a) Mrs Khandelwal had bought 3.5 kg of sugar. She put the sugar equally into 2 jars. How much sugar did she put in each jar?

3.5 ÷ 2 = ?

$$2\overline{)3.5}$$

$$\begin{array}{r} 1.7 \\ 2\overline{)3.5} \\ -2\downarrow \\ \hline 15 \\ 14 \\ \hline 1 \end{array}$$ ← **Remainder**

When you divide decimals, you **do not show remainders**. You have to **write extra zeros to complete the division.**

$$\begin{array}{r} 1.75 \\ 2\overline{)3.50} \\ -2\downarrow \\ \hline 15 \\ -14\downarrow \\ \hline 10 \\ 10 \\ \hline 0 \end{array}$$

Write an extra zero in the dividend to complete the division. This does not change the value of the dividend.

Answer: Each jar contains 1.75 kg of sugar.

1. Place the decimal points correctly in these quotients.

(a)
$$8\overline{)0.48} \quad 0\ 0\ 6$$

(b)
$$4\overline{)49.6} \quad 1\ 2\ 4$$

(c)
$$7\overline{)0.35} \quad 0\ 0\ 5$$

(d)
$$8\overline{)27.2} \quad 0\ 3\ 4$$

2. Divide. Check your answer with multiplication.

(a) $82.17 \div 9$ (b) $0.65 \div 5$ (c) $272.22 \div 6$ (d) $168.6 \div 3$

(e) $17.73 \div 3$ (f) $1.80 \div 5$ (g) $27.54 \div 9$ (h) $4.8 \div 12$

3. Divide until the remainder is zero.

(a) $90.3 \div 6$ (b) $17.2 \div 8$ (c) $3.1 \div 4$ (d) $9.15 \div 2$

(e) $7.4 \div 4$ (f) $5.2 \div 8$ (g) $2.67 \div 5$ (h) $18.9 \div 2$

Multiplying and Dividing Decimals by 10 and 100

- **Multiplying by 10 and 100**

  $3.92 \times 10 = 39.2$

  $0.39 \times 10 = 3.9$

  $3.92 \times 100 = 392.0 = 392$

  $0.3 \times 100 = 30.0\ = 30$

  ↑

  Write an extra zero
  to show the correct
  number of decimal places.

- To multiply a decimal by 10, move the point one place to the right.

- To multiply it by 100, move the point two places to the right.

Try This

(a) 0.78×10 (b) 0.7×100 (c) 1.3×10 (d) 1.32×100

Count the zeros to know
how many places to move.

- **Dividing by 10 and 100**
  $18.9 \div 10 = 1.89$
  $0.8 \div 10 = 0.08$

  ↑
  Write an extra zero to show the correct number of decimal places.
  ↓

  $8 \div 100 = 0.08$
  $18.9 \div 100 = 0.189$

- To divide a decimal by 10 move the point one place to the left.
- To divide it by 100 move the point two places to the left

This is the same as $8.0 \div 100$

I use this idea to remember in which direction to move the decimal point.

MR	Deepak	Lal
↓	↓	↓
Multiply Right	Divide	Left

Try This

(a) $42.8 \div 10$
(d) $42.8 \div 100$

(b) $725 \div 10$
(e) $725 \div 100$

(c) $0.9 \div 10$
(f) $9 \div 100$

Exercise 5.10

1. (a) 28.25×10 (b) 0.81×10 (c) 1.23×10 (d) 1.1×10
   (e) 16.73×100 (f) 3.19×100 (g) 0.14×100 (h) 0.8×100

2. (a) $5.76 \div 10$ (b) $8.3 \div 10$ (c) $0.9 \div 10$ (d) $36 \div 10$
   (e) $53.1 \div 100$ (f) $62 \div 100$ (g) $2.8 \div 100$ (h) $4 \div 100$

3. (a) $32.1 \times \underline{\quad} = 321$ (b) $15.26 \times \underline{\quad} = 152.6$ (c) $0.03 \times \underline{\quad} = 3$
   (d) $1.86 \times \underline{\quad} = 18.6$ (e) $1.75 \times \underline{\quad} = 175$ (f) $0.18 \times \underline{\quad} = 18$

4. (a) $0.6 \div \underline{\quad} = 0.06$ (b) $68.14 \div \underline{\quad} = 6.814$ (c) $31.6 \times \underline{\quad} = 3.16$
   (d) $0.91 \div \underline{\quad} = 0.091$ (e) $7 \div \underline{\quad} = 0.07$ (f) $1.1 \div \underline{\quad} = .011$

Connecting Decimals and Money

1 rupee = 100 p.
This can be shown using decimal representation as:

Re 1 = [grid of 100 p squares]

So

$$\frac{50}{100} \text{ rupee} = \frac{50}{100} = \text{Rs } 0.50$$

Therefore Re 1 Re 1 = Rs 1.50

In decimals = 1.50

(b) 75 p = $\frac{75}{100}$ rupee = Rs 0.75

In decimals = 0.75

Try This

Colour to show
Rs 0.25

Multiplying and Dividing with Money

Unitary Method

(a) Which is the better buy?

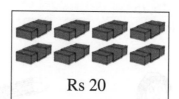

Rs 20

Rs 13.50

To find out compare the price of one blue eraser to the price of one pink eraser.
Price of one blue eraser Rs 20 ÷ 8 = ?

$8\overline{)20} \rightarrow$ $8\overline{)20.00} \rightarrow$ $8\overline{)20.00} \rightarrow$

$$\begin{array}{r} 2.50 \\ 8\overline{)20.00} \\ -16 \\ \hline 40 \\ -40 \\ \hline 00 \\ 00 \\ \hline 0 \end{array}$$

Common Mistake!

$$\begin{array}{r} 2.5 \\ 8\overline{)20.00} \\ -16 \\ \hline 40 \\ -40 \\ \hline 0 \end{array}$$

*The zero at the end
is important while
dividing money.*

One blue eraser costs Rs 2.50

Price of one pink eraser Rs 13.50 ÷ 6 = ?

```
        2.25
   6 ) 13.50          ⟶     One pink eraser costs Rs 2.25
     − 12
      ____
       15
     − 12
      ____
       30
       30
      ____
        0
```

The box of pink erasers is the better buy because one pink eraser is cheaper than one blue eraser.

Finding the 'price of one' is called finding the unit price for which we use the unitary method.

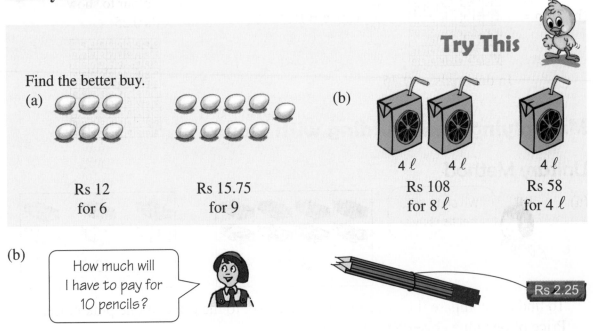

Try This

Find the better buy.

(a)

Rs 12 for 6   Rs 15.75 for 9

(b)

4 ℓ   4 ℓ   4 ℓ

Rs 108 for 8 ℓ   Rs 58 for 4 ℓ

(b)

How much will I have to pay for 10 pencils?

Rs 2.25

To find out how much 10 pencils will cost, you have to first find out the price of one pencil.

```
     0.75    One pencil costs Rs 0.75.
 3 ) 2.25
   − 2 1
    _____
     1 5    Now find out the cost of 10 pencils
   − 1 5    by multiplying.
    _____
       0    Rs 0.75 × 10 = Rs 7.50
            10 pencils will costs Rs 7.50.
```

Multiply like you normally multiply decimals.

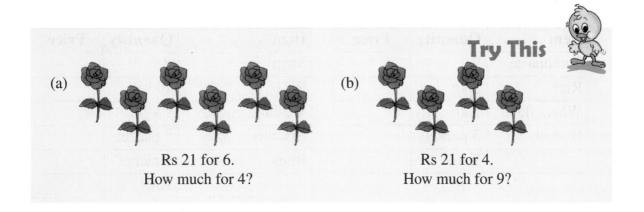

(a) Rs 21 for 6.
How much for 4?

(b) Rs 21 for 4.
How much for 9?

 **Exercise 5.11**

1. Here are some things needed to make a model air plane and their prices.

3 for | 2 for | 3 for | 1 for | 5 for
Rs 16.50 | Rs 23 | Rs 25.50 | Rs 12 | Rs 76.25

The pictures below show how many of each item Ranbir needs. How much will it cost him?

2. This is Mrs Viswanathan's grocery bill. First find the cost of one of each item then use the information to fill up the other two bills.

Item	Quantity	Price in rupees
Toothpaste	3	85.50
Soap	4	60.00
Rice	8 kg	202.00
Wheat flour	10 kg	185.00
Washing powder	2 kg	86.00
Biscuits	6 packets	70.50
Buns	10 pieces	42.00
	Total	731.00

Item	Quantity	Price
Toothpaste	2	
Rice	5 kg	
Wheat flour	5 kg	
Biscuits	3 packets	
	Total	

Item	Quantity	Price
Soap	2	
Rice	10 kg	
Washing powder	1 kg	
Biscuits	5 packets	
Buns	6 pieces	
	Total	

Project

10 students from the class who live in different areas should find the price of a kilo of potatoes, onions, and tomatoes in their area. They should also find out whether it is cheaper to buy a larger quantity. How much would it cost then? Compare the prices per kilo. What is the saving per kilo?

Problem Solving

Using Strategies—Systematic Trials

Some problems need you to try out different solutions in a systematic manner in order to be able to arrive at the right one.

Problem: Anisha had Rs 10.50 with her. She bought some pencils costing Rs 2.50 each and some erasers costing Rs 1.00 each. If she bought 6 items altogether, how many of each did she buy?

We need to find out how many pencils and how many erasers Anisha bought.
We can find the solution by using all the possible combinations that make 6 items and then finding out the cost.

Pencils + Erasers	Cost (in rupees)
1 + 5	Cost $(1 \times 2.50) + (5 \times 1.00)$ $2.50 + 5.00 = 7.50$
2 + 4	Cost $(2 \times 2.50) + (4 \times 1.00)$ $5.00 + 4.00 = 9.00$
3 + 3	Cost $(3 \times 2.50) + (3 \times 1.00)$ $7.50 + 3.00 = 10.50$

The last solution is the correct one as the cost works out to Rs 10.50 for 6 items.
Answer: Anisha bought 3 pencils and 3 erasers.

Exercise 5.12

Use systematic trials to solve.

1. The Sethi family spends Rs 12 on 4 tickets for entrance to the school fete. The adult tickets cost Rs 3.50 and the children's tickets cost Rs 1.50. How many of each did they buy?

2. Sangeeta sold 15 packets of popcorn at the fete. Large packets were sold at Rs 5.25 and the smaller ones cost Rs 3. If Sangeeta collected Rs 63, how many of each did she sell?

3. A toy car costs Rs 50 and a toy truck costs Rs 65. Sushil bought 6 of them as prizes for his stall at the fete. If he spent Rs 330, how many of each item did he buy?

4. The school canteen bought 16 new trays. Red trays cost Rs 15.75 and blue trays cost Rs 13.25. If Rs 232 was spent in all, how many of each was bought?

5. Two types of lucky draw coupons were being sold at the fete at Rs 7.50 and Rs 10 each. Arjun sold 8 coupons and collected Rs 67.50. How many of each type did he sell?

CHAPTER CHECK-UP

1. **Add.**
   (a) $300 + 7 + 0.09$
   (b) $0.7 + 0.06$
   (c) $10 + 7 + \dfrac{3}{100}$
   (d) $600 + 6 + \dfrac{2}{100}$

2. **Compare using <, >, or =.**
   (a) $4.09 \bigcirc 40.09$
   (b) $0.78 \bigcirc 0.09$
   (c) $3.84 \bigcirc 3.08$
   (d) $5 \bigcirc 2.1$

3. **Arrange in ascending order.**
   (a) 13.19   1.319   131.9   13.09
   (b) 40   40.6   4.06   40.01

4. **Arrange in descending order.**
   (a) 3.07   3.079   3.013   3.8
   (b) 8.11   8.01   8.101   8.1

4. **Solve.**
   (a) $5.2 + 3.67$
   (b) $16.95 + 12$
   (c) $28.1 - 16.25$
   (d) $3 - 1.1$
   (e) 0.04×2
   (f) $9.25 \div 5$
   (g) $8.79 \div 3$
   (h) 85.7×100
   (i) $961 \div 100$
   (j) 9.2×10
   (k) $2.9 \div 10$

5. 9 icecreams cost Rs 67.50. What will 10 icecreams cost?

6. A packet of 4 notebooks costs Rs 30. How much will one notebook cost?

7.  6 kg of grapes cost Rs 195. How much will 17 kg cost?

8. 3 kg of peanuts cost Rs 76.50. How much will 1 kg cost?

9. Mrs Swaroop bought 6.25 m of dress material for her older daughter, and 5.75 m for the younger one. How many metres of dress material did Mrs Swaroop buy?

10. The winning team for the march past scored 8.7, 6.2, and 9.25 points from three different judges. What was their total score?

11. An adult's toothbrush is 15.5 cm long and a child's toothbrush is 13.7 cm long. How much longer is an adult's toothbrush?

WORKSHEET

You know that like we have rupees in India, other countries have other currencies.

The chart below shows how many Indian rupees are equal to one unit of a foriegn currency on a particular day. Use the chart to answer the questions.

Country	Currency	Indian Rupees
Japan	1 Yen	Rs 0.40
USA	1 Dollar	Rs 42.85
China	1 Yuan	Rs 6.20
U.K.	1 Pound	Rs 83.90
France	1 Euro	Rs 66.39
Malaysia	1 Ringgit	Rs 13.14
Pakistan	1 Rupee	Rs 0.63
Russia	1 Rouble	Rs 1.81

1. How many Indian rupees will you get for 100 U.S. dollars?

2. On his visit to Moscow, Shishir bought a gift for 50 roubles. How much is that in Indian rupees?

3. What costs more? 1000 pounds or 1000 euros? How much more?
   (*Hint:* Convert both to Indian rupees and then compare.)

4. Who earns more? A man who earns 2000 Pakistani rupees in Pakistan or a man who earns 1000 roubles in Russia?

5. Amartya buys a watch for Ringgit 200 in Malaysia. How much is that in Indian rupees?

Keeping in Touch

1. Find the HCF using prime factorisation.
   (a) 12, 36   (b) 15, 30, 25
2. Find the LCM using prime factorisation.
   (a) 24, 36   (b) 14, 21, 42

MATHS LAB ACTIVITY

Converting Decimals

Objective: To reinforce conversion of decimals to fractions and vice versa.

Materials Required: Cards of 4 cm × 8 cm

Preparation: Fill in the following decimals and fractions on the cards. Students play in pairs with one complete set of 20 cards.

$\frac{1}{10}$, 0.1, $\frac{1}{10}$, 0.01, $\frac{2}{10}$, 0.2, $\frac{2}{100}$, 0.02, 0.3, 0.30

0.03, $\frac{3}{100}$, 0.4, $\frac{4}{10}$, 0.04, 0.5, 0.50, $\frac{5}{100}$, 0.05, $\frac{4}{100}$

Steps:

1. The students must first shuffle all 20 cards. They then spread them out and place them face down.
2. Now they take turns to turn over any two cards at a time.
3. If the cards match, the student can keep the cards. If they do not match, they are put back in the same place.
4. The game is over when all the cards have been collected. The student with most cards wins the game.

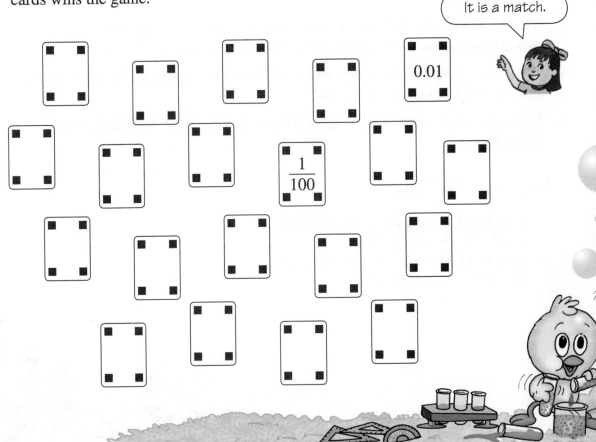

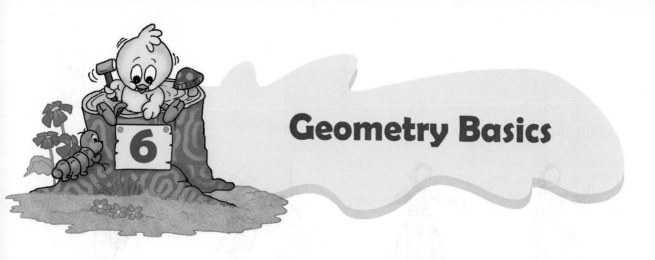

Geometry Basics

Recognising Angles

Put these closed shapes into two groups. Colour the shapes with straight lines in yellow and the shapes with curved lines in blue.

Angles

All the shapes you have coloured above in yellow are called polygons and their sides meet at corners.

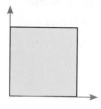  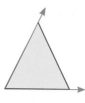

The two sides that meet at a corner form an angle.

We see angles around us all the time.

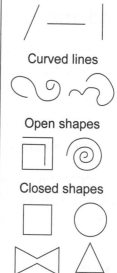

Straight lines
/ — |
Curved lines
Open shapes
Closed shapes

Mark the angles that you can see in these dance forms.

| Lavani | Kathak | Dandiya Rass | Bharatnatyam |

Understanding Angles in Geometric Terms

To understand angles in geometric terms, we must first understand some of these basic concepts that are also called the building blocks of geometry.

Point

A point is the basic unit of geometry. It shows an exact location.

We represent a point with the help of a dot and name it with a capital letter.

• A   This is point A.

The tip of a pin can be taken as a physical model of a point. In reality, a point in geometry is even smaller than the tip of a pin.

Line

A line is a collection of points going endlessly in both directions along a straight path.

A line has no beginning and no end, so it has no end points. It is named by using two points on it. The symbol for a line is ←——→. The arrows show that the line goes on and on.

A   B

Point A and Point B are two points on the line. We call it line AB and write it as $\overleftrightarrow{AB}$ or $\overleftrightarrow{BA}$.

When you stand at the seashore the horizon gives you the idea of a never-ending line.

Line segment

A line segment is part of a line. It has two endpoints. We name it by its endpoints. The symbol for a line segment is ——

The edge of your blackboard in class can be taken as a physical representation of a line segment. It has a definite starting point and ending point.

Points M and N are the two endpoints of the line segment MN. We write it as $\overline{MN}$ or $\overline{NM}$

Ray

A ray is part of a line. It has one endpoint and goes on endlessly in one direction.

The symbol for a ray is →

Ray PQ is written as $\overrightarrow{PQ}$

A beam of light from a torch in a dark room can be compared to a ray. It has a definite endpoint and goes on continuously in one direction.

Try This

Which geometrical concept does each of these remind you?

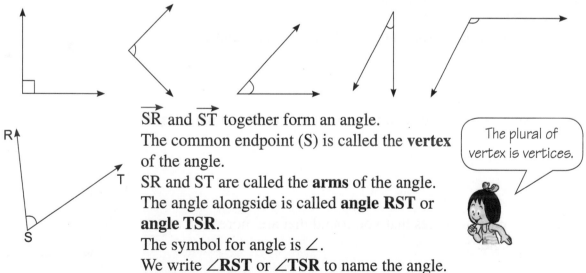

| Imagine a never ending clothes line | The tip of a needle | The rays of the sun | The edge of this book |

Parts of an Angle

When two rays have a common endpoint they form an angle.

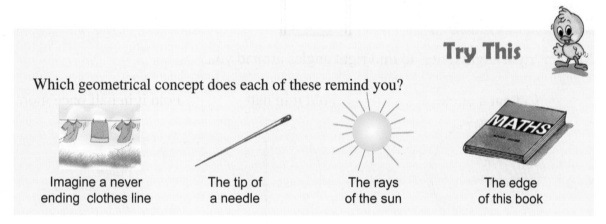

$\overrightarrow{SR}$ and $\overrightarrow{ST}$ together form an angle.
The common endpoint (S) is called the **vertex** of the angle.
SR and ST are called the **arms** of the angle.
The angle alongside is called **angle RST** or **angle TSR**.
The symbol for angle is ∠.
We write ∠**RST** or ∠**TSR** to name the angle.

The plural of vertex is vertices.

The middle letter is always the vertex of the angle.

Types of Angles

Right angles

Angles that look like the corners of this page are called **right angles**.

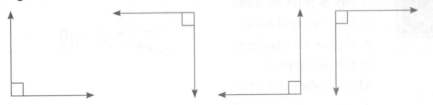

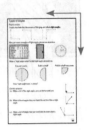

Here are some examples of right angles that we see around us.

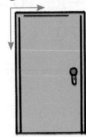

March 2009					
Monday	30	2	9	16	23
Tuesday	31	3	10	17	24
Wednesday		4	11	18	25
Thursday		5	12	19	26
Friday		6	13	20	27
Saturday		7	14	21	28
Sunday	1	8	15	22	29

Make a 'right angle tester' to find right angles around you.

Cut out a circle	Fold it in half	Fold it in half once more

Your 'right angle tester' is ready!

Use the tester to:

(a) Make a list of the right angles you can find around you.

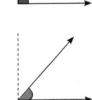

(b) Make a list of angles that you found that are less than a right angle.

(c) Make a list of angles that you found that are more than a right angle.

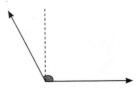

How many right angles can you find in this diagram of a tennis court?

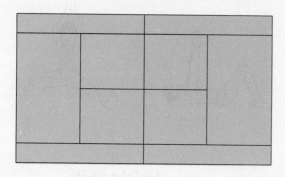

(*Hint:* There are more than 30 but less than 50.)

Acute, Obtuse, and Straight Angles

Acute angles

Angles that are less than a right angle are called **acute** angles.

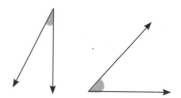

Here are some examples of acute angles that we see around us.

Obtuse angles

Angles that are more than a right angle are called **obtuse** angles.

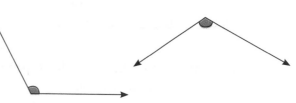

Here are some examples of obtuse angles that we see around us.

  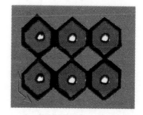 

Mark the acute angles in blue and the obtuse angles in green on these pictures of yoga postures.

Straight angles

If you have two right angles next to one another, they form a **straight angle**.

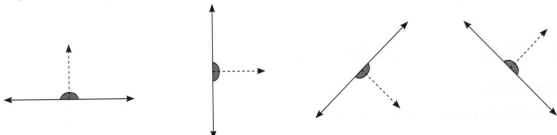

Here are some examples of straight angles that we see around us.

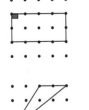 **Exercise 6.1**

1. **In the figures given below colour the right angles in red, the acute angles in blue, and the obtuse angles in green. Some are done for you.**

  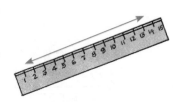 

2. The pictures you see below is a signalling system called 'semaphore' which was used by the navy. Name the angle that each signal forms.

3. Draw three examples (objects) each of acute, obtuse, and right angles that you see around you.

4. Identify the following angles.

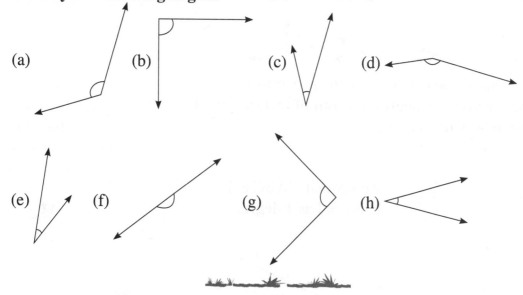

(a) (b) (c) (d)

(e) (f) (g) (h)

Project

Write the names of all the members of your family using straight lines. Find out how many right, acute, obtuse, or straight angles are there in each name.

Right angles	2
Obtuse angles	4
Acute angles	8
Straight angles	1

Challenge

This picture shows some of the angles a striker can make on a carrom board.
Name all the angles shown in the picture. You should get 10 angles.

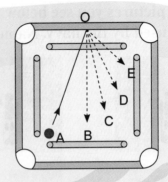

1.   2.   3.   4.   5.
6.   7.   8.   9.   10.

Measuring Angles

Use two pencils to represent the arms of an angle. Slowly move one pencil as shown. See how the gap between the two pencils slowly increases.

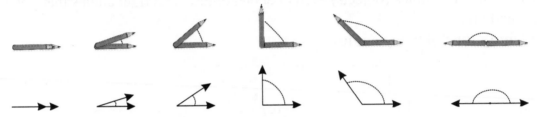

We can measure the gap between the two arms of the angle by using 'degrees'. **A degree is a unit of measurement used for measuring angles.**

> The length of the arms does not affect the measure of the angle.

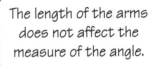

We say that ∠ABC is 1°.
1° is read as 1 degree.

∠XYZ = 10°

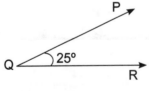

∠PQR = 25°

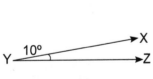

∠LMN = 90°

You can use a **protractor** to measure angles.
If you look at a protractor carefully, you will see that there are two sets of measurements written on it.
These are called **scales**.
There is an **inner scale** and an **outer scale**, both having 0° to 180° in different directions.

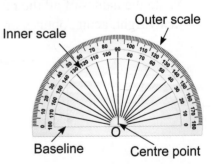

This is how a protractor is used to measure angles.

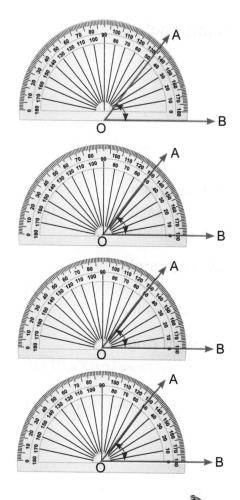

Step 1: Place the centre point of the protractor on the vertex of the angle.

Step 2: Adjust the protractor (without shifting the centre from the vertex) so that one arm of the angle is along the baseline.

Step 3: Look at the scale where the baseline arm points to 0° (inner scale in this example).

Step 4: Read the measure of this angle where the other arm crosses the scale.

Answer: ∠AOB = 50°.

Try This

Use a protractor to measure this right angle. What did you get?

Project

Make a chart showing the physical exercises that you have learnt in school. Mark out the angles that you can make with your body. Use simple stick figures and measure the angles.

115

Right angle

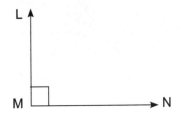

$\angle LMN = 90°$
A 90° angle is a **right angle**.

A right angle is represented as

Acute angle

An acute angle is smaller than a right angle; so it is **more than 0°ut less than 90°**.

Obtuse angle

An obtuse angle is bigger than a right angle; so it is **more than 90° but less than 180°**.

Straight angle

It is the same as **two right angles**. So **it measures exactly 180°**.

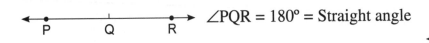

$\angle PQR = 180° =$ Straight angle

Try This

Take a square piece of paper (a) and fold it in half (b). Fold it once more (c) and press down. Open the last fold so that the sheet of paper shows the crease (d). Take one corner of the paper and get it to meet the crease line (e).

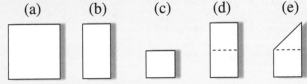

(a)   (b)   (c)   (d)   (e)

You now have an acute angle, a right angle, an obtuse angle, and a straight angle. Measure each of them with a protractor.

Common Mistake!

You can avoid this mistake by first observing the angle and deciding what kind of angle it is—obtuse or acute.
Secondly, always use the scale where the baseline arm points to zero.

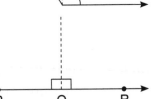

$\angle ABC = 45°$ ✗
$\angle ABC = 135°$ ✓

1. **What is the measure of these angles?**

   (a)
   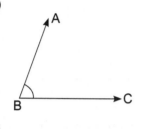

   (b)
   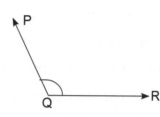

   (c)
   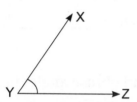

   (d)
   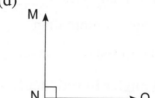

2. **Measure these angles with your protractor. Then state what type of angles they are.**

   (a)
   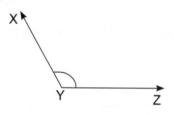

   (b)
   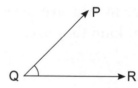

   (c)
   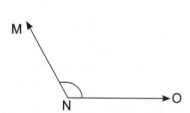

   (d)
   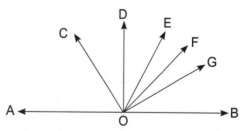

   Use a protractor to measure the angles in part (d).

   ∠AOC =   ∠AOE =   ∠AOG =   ∠AOB =

   ∠BOD =   ∠BOF =   ∠BOG =   ∠BOC =

3. Draw 10 different angles with a ruler in your notebook. Then measure them with your protractor.

CHAPTER CHECK-UP

1. **Fill in the blanks.**

   (a) A ray extends endlessly in _____ direction.

   (b) You cannot measue a ray and a _____ .

   (c) A part of a line that has two endpoints is a _____.

   (d) An angle that looks like the corner of a cupboard is a _____ .

   (e) An angle is formed by two _____ having a common endpoint.

   (f) An obtuse angle is more than _____° and less than _____°.

   (g) An angle that measures 1° is an _____ angle.

2. **Mark the right angles in red, acute angles in blue, and obtuse angles in green.**

3. **Use a protractor to measure the angles from (a) to (i) in these two figures, and then name what kind they are.**

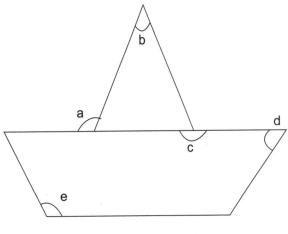

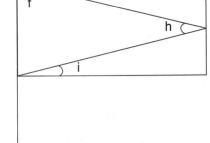

   (a)   (b)   (c)

   (d)   (e)   (f)

   (g)   (h)   (i)

WORKSHEET

Give the approximate measurement of these angles.

_____

_____

_____

_____

_____

_____

_____

_____

_____

Use this guide to help you.

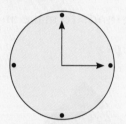

3 o'clock = 90°

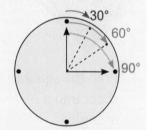

90 ÷ 3 = 30°

The angle formed between any two consecutive numbers on the clock face is 30°.

Keeping in Touch

(a) $2\frac{3}{5} + 1\frac{6}{7}$ (b) $\frac{5}{7} - \frac{3}{8}$ (c) $\frac{7}{8} \times \frac{3}{5}$ (d) $\frac{3}{7} \div \frac{9}{11}$

MATHS LAB ACTIVITY

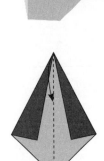

Objective: To create and recognise angles through paper folding.

Materials Required: Square sheet of origami paper
(about 12 cm × 12 cm) with one side white and one side black.

Preparation: None

Method: To make an origami penguin.

Steps:

1. Fold the square sheet into a triangle.

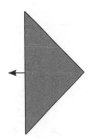

2. Open the triangle.

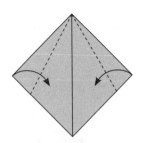

3. Fold the sides as shown. Corners should not touch the centre crease.

4. Fold the top as shown

5. Turn over the paper.

6. Fold the point up as shown.

7. Fold the paper in half.

8. Lift the head up as shown.

Your penguin is ready.

Record the activity:

1. How many right, acute, and obtuse angles can you see in the penguin?

2. Open up the sheet and note all the creases. Mark the right, acute, and obtuse angles that you see. Measure a few of them with a protractor.

TEST YOUR SKILLS*

1. (a) $\frac{8}{11} + \frac{3}{11} + \frac{6}{11}$ (b) $2\frac{1}{3} - 1\frac{5}{6}$ (c) $6 \times \frac{3}{4}$

   (d) $\frac{3}{7} \times \frac{4}{3}$ (e) $\frac{11}{13} \div 7$ (f) $\frac{6}{11} \div \frac{3}{5}$

2. (a) **Put in ascending order.**   (b) **Put in descending order.**

   $\frac{5}{6}$ $\frac{3}{4}$ $\frac{1}{2}$ $\frac{8}{9}$ $\frac{3}{5}$ $\frac{2}{3}$ $\frac{7}{9}$ $\frac{6}{7}$

3. (a) $5.2 + 3.53$ (b) $7 - 1.95$ (c) 8.1×3

   (d) 18.3×100 (e) $76.5 \div 100$ (f) $13.5 \div 9$

4. (a) **Put in ascending order.**   (b) **Put in descending order.**

   5.07, 5.17, 5.71, 5.70   6.13, 6.3, 6.1, 6.31

5. (a) 8 kg of mangoes cost Rs 364. How much does 1 kg cost?
   (b) One candle costs Rs 5.25. How much will 12 candles cost?

6. **There are six line segments here. Can you find and name them all?**

   R   S   T   U

7. **Use a protractor to measure these angles and say what kind each is.**

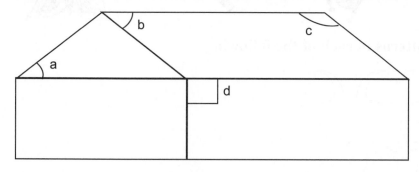

   (a) ____° _____ angle
   (b) ____° _____ angle
   (c) ____° _____ angle
   (d) ____° _____ angle

Exploring Shapes and Patterns

7

 Looking Back

1. Ring the shapes that do not have symmetry.

2. Draw the line of symmetry for these shapes.

3. Complete the patterns in each of the following.

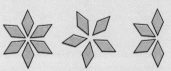

Symmetry

Line of Symmetry

The Charminar in Hyderabad is a symmetrical monument because one half is a **reflection** of the other half.

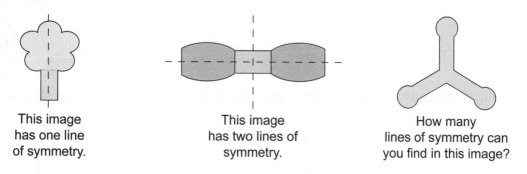

This image has one line of symmetry.	This image has two lines of symmetry.	How many lines of symmetry can you find in this image?

The dotted lines here are not lines of symmetry.

The shape alone does not give symmetry. The details within the shape also decide whether the shape is symmetrical or not.

Try This

Tick (✓) the images that have symmetry and draw their line or lines of symmetry.

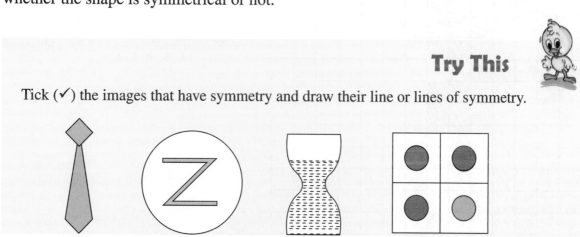

The line of symmetry shows where the shape has been reflected.
You can take any shape drawn on a piece of paper and make it a symmetrical shape with the help of a mirror.

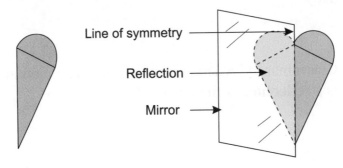

Line of symmetry

Reflection

Mirror

Try This

Put a mirror along the red line and draw the reflection to create a symmetrical shape.

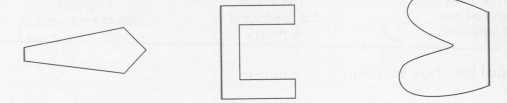

Kullu Valley in Himachal Pradesh is famous for its woollen shawls with traditional border designs. Colour the other half of this square by reflecting the design to make a basic Kullu shawl border pattern.

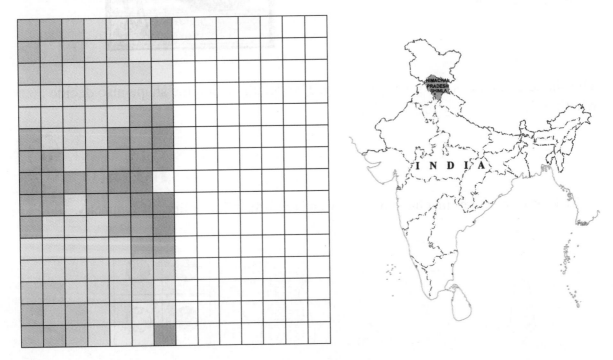

1. Draw the lines of symmetry for these shapes.

    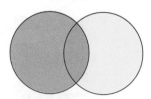

2. Look at these flags and say whether they have 0, 1, or 2 lines of symmetry.

(a)

Australian flag ☐

(b)

United Kingdom flag ☐

(c)

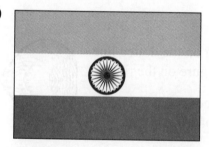

Indian flag ☐

(d)

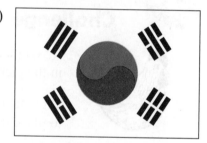

South Korean flag ☐

(e)

Canadian flag ☐

(f)

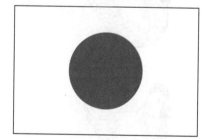

Japanese flag ☐

3. Use a mirror on the red line to draw the reflection of the shape.

   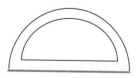  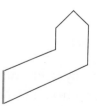

4. Traditionally, people decorate eggs for the festival of Easter. Draw a design on one side of the egg and use a mirror on the line of symmetry to copy the reflection on the other side. One has been partly done for you.

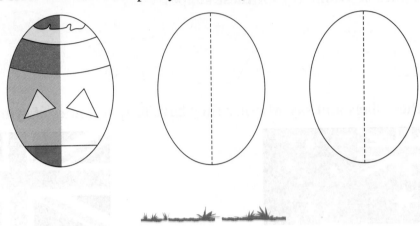

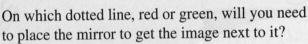

Challenge

If you place a mirror facing you on the dotted line in the picture you will get the figure on the right.

On which dotted line, red or green, will you need to place the mirror to get the image next to it?

Project

Draw any interesting shape of your own. Use a mirror to create new symmetrical pictures from it. Challenge a friend to find the line of symmetry.

Turning Shapes

Quarter Turn

This design can be found on the floor of the Taj Mahal. It has been made by turning shapes.

In the design, has been turned to make .

If we put a dot on the shape and then turn it, we can see that it has been turned $\frac{1}{4}$ or quarter turn.

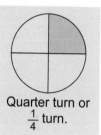

Quarter turn or $\frac{1}{4}$ turn.

There are some special shapes that look the same even we give them a quarter turn. The dot on the shape below will help you see that.

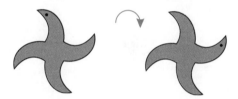

Complete this pattern using quarter turns. The first quarter turn has ben outlined for you.

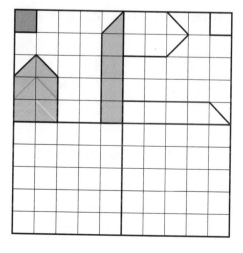

Try This

Tick the shape that will look the same after a quarter turn.

Use a tracing paper to trace these shapes. Then turn the tracing paper $\frac{1}{4}$ turn over the original shape to decide.

Half Turn

Some shapes look the same after a half turn.

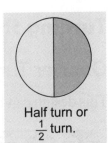

Half turn or
$\frac{1}{2}$ turn.

Look at this design.

Quarter turn
Does not
look the same

Half turn
Look the same

Try This

Which of these shapes will look the
same on a $\frac{1}{2}$ turn?

Use a trick! Turn the page upside
down if you want to know how a shape
will look after a $\frac{1}{2}$ turn.

Exercise 7.2

1. **Which of these shapes will look the same after $\frac{1}{4}$ turn? Put a tick mark (✓) next to it.**

   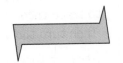

2. **Which of these shapes will look the same after $\frac{1}{2}$ turn? Put a tick mark (✓) next to it.**

3. **Draw how these shapes will look after these turns. Tick (✓) those look the same after the turn.**

Shapes	$\frac{1}{4}$ turn	$\frac{1}{2}$ turn

4. Which 6 letters of the English alphabet look the same after half a turn?

5. **Circle the numbers that look the same on half a turn.**

   11,   88,   18,   808,   118,   818,   1001,   1100,   1881

6. Which is the largest 4-digit number you can make that will look the same on a $\frac{1}{2}$ turn? Which is the smallest?

7. **Change the shape so that the new shape looks the same on a $\frac{1}{2}$ turn. The first one has been done for you.**

(a)  changed to    (b)   (c)   (d)

Project

Many crosswords have the same shape when turned. Go through newspapers to find such crosswords and paste them in your notebook in columns. Show how many turns they need to come back to their original position. Ignore those that need a full turn.

One-third Turn

This is the hub cap of a car wheel.

 It will look the same after $\frac{1}{3}$ turn.

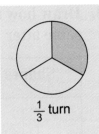

$\frac{1}{3}$ turn

Try This

Which of these internationally recognised environmental symbols are the same after a $\frac{1}{3}$ turn? Put a tick mark (✓) next to it.

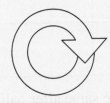

Save planet earth!

Recycle   Reuse   Reduce

One-sixth Turn

This is the steering wheel of a ship.

 If you give it a $\frac{1}{6}$ turn, it will look the same.

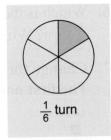

$\frac{1}{6}$ turn

Try This

Which of these shapes will look the same after a $\frac{1}{6}$ turn? Put tick mark (✓) next to it.

          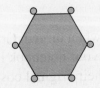

Exercise 7.3

1. Write $\frac{1}{3}$ or $\frac{1}{6}$ according to the turn these shapes need to come back to their original shapes.

(a) 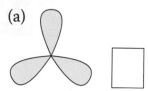 ☐

(b) 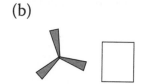 ☐

(c)  ☐

(d) 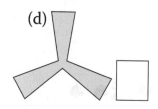 ☐

(e) 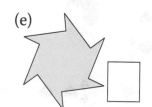 ☐

(f) 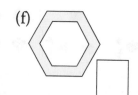 ☐

(g) 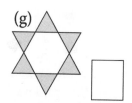 ☐

2. Draw these shapes after $\frac{1}{3}$ and $\frac{1}{6}$ turns. Tick mark (✓) those that come back to their original shapes.

Shapes	$\frac{1}{3}$ turn	$\frac{1}{6}$ turn

Project

Go through magazines and newspapers and cut out logos and symbols that you find. Sort them into those which come back to their original shape on $\frac{1}{4}$, $\frac{1}{2}$, $\frac{1}{3}$, or $\frac{1}{6}$ turns. Ignore those that need a full turn to come back to their original shapes.

Challenge

This set has 4 playing cards kept in a row.

One card has been rotated at $\frac{1}{2}$ turn in this set.

Which card has been turned?

Creating Patterns

This pattern has been created by repeating the same design over and over again without any change.

If we take the basic design and rotate it by $\frac{1}{2}$ turn, we can create a new pattern by repeating the two designs.

What happens when we repeat a basic design with a $\frac{1}{4}$ turn every time?

Try This

First create a pattern by repeating the design.

Now complete the new pattern by rotating it by $\frac{1}{2}$ a turn every time.

Now complete the pattern by turning it $\frac{1}{4}$ turn every time.

Use tracing paper to copy and then repeat or rotate.

Exercise 7.4

1. **Use the designs shown below and create three sets of patterns for each as mentioned with the help of tracing paper in your notebooks.**

   (a) 　　(b) 　　(c)

   (i) Repeat the design.

   (ii) Repeat by giving a $\frac{1}{2}$ turn every time.

   (iii) Repeat by giving a $\frac{1}{4}$ turn every time.

2. **Complete the patterns using turns as shown till you come back to the first position.**

3. These patterns have been made by moving the designs anti-clockwise. What will come next?

(a)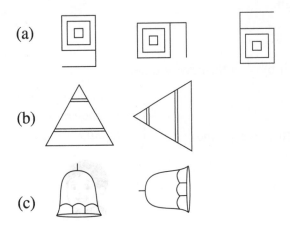

(b)

(c)

4. Spot the pattern and continue.

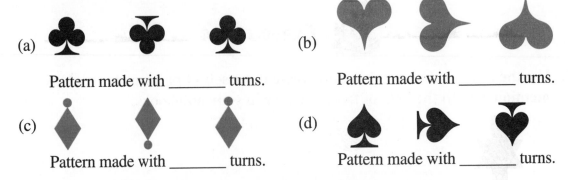

(a)

Pattern made with _____ turns.

(b)

Pattern made with _____ turns.

(c)

Pattern made with _____ turns.

(d)

Pattern made with _____ turns.

5. Circle the design that breaks the pattern and then set it right.

(a)

(b)

(c)

6. Complete the designs on the plates.

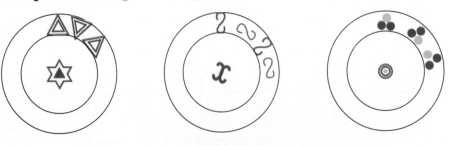

CHAPTER CHECK-UP

1. Which of these are lines of symmetry?

(a)   (b)   (c)   (d)   (e)  (f)

2. Decide which need $\frac{1}{2}$ turn and $\frac{1}{4}$ turn to come back to their original shape.

(a)   (b)   (c)   (d)   (e)   (f)

3. Which of these need $\frac{1}{3}$ turn and which need $\frac{1}{6}$ turn to come back to their original shape.

(a)   (b)   (c)   (d)   (e)   (f)

4. Complete the pattern till it comes back to its original position.

(a)

(b)

(c) 3 3 3

WORKSHEET

This worksheet integrates Maths and EVS.

Number	Traffic sign	Meaning	Symmetry Yes/No	Looks the same on a turn* Yes/No	Kind of turn needed $\frac{1}{4}$, $\frac{1}{2}$, $\frac{1}{3}$, or $\frac{1}{6}$
(a)		No stopping or Standing			
(b)		No parking			
(c)		Compulsory ahead			
(d)		Stop			
(e)		Round about			
(f)		Give way			

* Ignore full turns.

Keeping in Touch

(a) 2.8×10
(b) 7.61×100
(c) 5.2×3
(d) $3.15 \div 5$
(e) $86.1 \div 10$
(f) $93 \div 100$

MATHS LAB ACTIVITY

Objective: To reinforce the concept of rotation.

Materials Required: Map of India, tracing paper, dark pencil, plain paper

Preparation: Students work independently or in pairs.

Steps:

1. The students use the map of India to trace out the shape of any state they like.
2. The student then carefully turns the tracing paper through a half or a quarter turn and creates a **rotated shape** of the state.
3. Both the students now stick the rotated shapes on a fresh sheet of paper. Then they go around asking their classmates to guess the state on their sheet. In turn they too try to name the states that the others have traced.

Try this out:

Identify these states.

This activity integrates Maths and Geography.

LOOKING BEYOND

Enrichment Time

This shape has been made with 5 cubes.
A mirror kept on the red line facing left will
create a reflected shape like the one shown.
Take a mirror and keep it on the dotted line.
Then match the shape with the correct line
of symmetry to the reflected shape below.

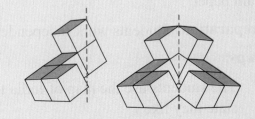

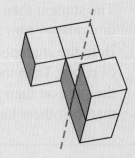

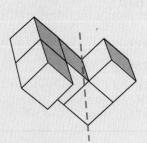

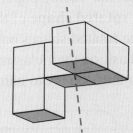

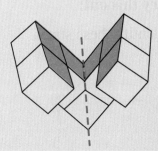

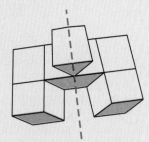

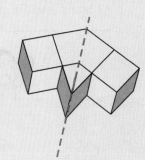

Activity Bag

Create a symmetrical picture with a friend. Take a 10 × 10 squared sheet of
paper and divide it into two halves. Use a colour pencil to fill in any square in
your half. Your friend must now fill in the corresponding square on his half,
using the same colour. Then he fills in a new square on his half which you must
reflect on your half. In the end you would have created a pattern with
line symmetry.

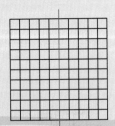

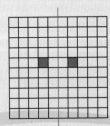

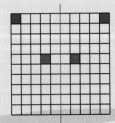

Measurement

Looking Back

Length
It takes Paresh 10 minutes to walk **1 kilometre (km)**.
1 km = 1000 metre (m)
1 m = 100 centimetre (cm)

About 1 m

Breadth of a finger is about 1 cm

Mass

We use **kilograms (kg)** to weigh heavier objects and **grams (g)** to weigh lighter ones.
1 kg = 1000 g

About 1 g   About 1 kg

Capacity
Litre (ℓ) is used to measure larger quantities of liquid and **millilitres (mℓ)** is used to measure smaller quantities of liquid.
1 ℓ = 1000 mℓ

Holds about 5 mℓ of water

Holds about 1 ℓ of water

Convert the following.

(a) 300 cm = _____ m   (b) 5 m = _____ cm   (c) 8000 g = _____ kg

(d) 4 kg = _____ g   (e) 2000 mℓ = _____ ℓ   (f) 9 ℓ = _____ mℓ

(g) 7500 g = _____ kg   (h) $3\frac{1}{2}$ ℓ = _____ mℓ   (i) 2520 m = __ km __ m

Measurement of Length

If you were asked to measure the lead tip of your pencil, what would you use?

A centimetre is too big to measure my pencil point!

So you need a smaller unit of measurement.

If a centimetre is further put into 10 equal parts, each part is called a millimetre (mm).

10 mm

0   1   2 cm

1 cm = 10 mm

1 mm

0   1   2 cm

$1 \text{ mm} = \frac{1}{10}$ cm

The breadth of the hour hand of your watch is about 1 mm.

1 mm = 0.1 cm using decimals.

 → 5 mm or 0.5 cm

We use millimetres to measure very small lengths or when we want to measure longer lengths with greater accuracy.

The diameter of this 5-rupee coin is about 2 cm 3 mm.

Using the smaller unit it is 23 mm.
(2 cm × 10 = 20 mm + 3 mm)
Using decimals we can write this as 2.3 cm using the bigger unit.
(23 ÷ 10 = 2.3 cm)

To change mm to cm ÷ by 10. To change cm to mm × by 10.

Common Mistake!

2 cm 3 mm
2.3 mm ✘
2.3 cm ✔

Try This

(a) Take a grain of rice and measure its length to the nearest mm.

(b) Find a bangle and measure its thickness to the nearest mm.

(c) 5.1 cm = _____ mm

(d) 15 mm = _____ cm

Exercise 8.1

1. **Measure. Give your answer in (a) cm and mm, (b) cm, (c) mm.**

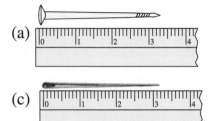

(a)

(b)

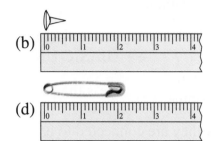

(c)

(d)

2. **Use your ruler to measure the wing span of the butterfly at the marked lines.**

Top = _____ cm _____ mm or _____ cm

Middle = _____ cm _____ mm or _____ cm

Bottom = _____ cm _____ mm or _____ cm

3. **Match the following.**

3.8 cm	50 mm
38 mm	0.5 cm
38 cm	3.8 cm
5 mm	3 cm 8 mm
5 cm	380 mm

4. (a) Measure the length of each finger and each fingernail shown in the picture here.
   (b) Trace out your hand on a sheet of paper and measure the length of each finger.

Project

Take coins of different denominations. Measure their diameters to the nearest mm. Record the findings in your notebook by outlining the coins with a pencil and writing the diameter next to each.

Relating Different Units of Length

You have now learnt four units of measurement of length. They are given below in order from big to small.

Kilometre (km) → more than a metre
Metre (m) → BASIC UNIT OF LENGTH
Centimetre (cm) ⎫
Millimetre (mm) ⎭ less than a metre

Let us see how they are connected to each other in the place-value system.

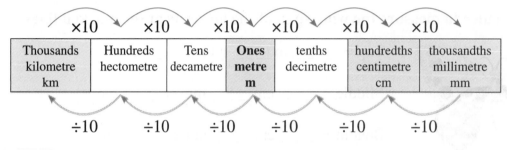

×10	×10	×10	×10	×10	×10	
Thousands kilometre km	Hundreds hectometre	Tens decametre	**Ones metre m**	tenths decimetre	hundredths centimetre cm	thousandths millimetre mm

÷10   ÷10   ÷10   ÷10   ÷10   ÷10

Every move to the right makes the unit 10 times smaller.

Multiply to change from a bigger unit to a smaller unit.

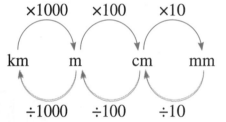

×1000   ×100   ×10

km   m   cm   mm

÷1000   ÷100   ÷10

Divide to change from a smaller unit to a bigger unit.

Remember

1 km = 1000 m
1 m = 100 cm
1 cm = 10 mm

1 m = ? mm
This can be written as
$1\,m = 100\,cm = 100 \times 10\,mm = 1000\,mm$

Common Mistake!

5 m 20 cm
= 5.20 cm ✗
= 5.20 m ✓

Using Decimals to Express Length

We can use decimals to express length.
The giraffe is 5 m 20 cm tall.
We can express this length in the larger unit using decimals as 5.20 m.
We can express this in the smaller units as 520 cm.

Project

Find out your height and the height of the members of your family. Express it in cm and then in m. Who is the tallest? Who is the shortest?

Converting from One Unit to Another

(a) If each ant is 8 mm in length, how long is the line in cm?

$11 \times 8 = 88$ mm is the length of the line in mm.

88 mm = _____?_____ cm

mm is the smaller unit and cm is the bigger unit. The rule says Small to Big Divide (SBD).

$88 \div 10 = 8.8$ cm

The line is 8.8 cm long.

(b)  A king cobra can be 3.6 m long. How many cm is that?

3.6 m = _____ cm

The rule says Big to Small Multiply (BSM).

$3.6 \times 100 = 360$ cm

The snake is 360 cm long.

(c) A grasshopper which can go 25 cm with one hop would have gone how many metres in 75 hops?

75×25 cm = 1875 cm would have been covered.

1875 cm = _____?_____ m

$1875 \div 100 = 18.75$ m

The grasshopper would have gone 18.75 m.

(d) A pile of 100 *chapattis* is 21 cm. How thick is 1 *chapatti* in mm?

$21 \times 10 = 210$ mm → To find the thickness of the pile in mm

$210 \div 100 = 2.1$ → To find the thickness of one *chapatti*

BSM rule for conversion from cm to mm.

One *chapatti* is 2.1 mm.

(e) Renee walks 5500 m every morning. How many km is that?

5500 m = _____ km

$5500 \div 1000 = 5.5$ km

Use the SBD rule to convert m to km.

Renee would have walked 5.5 km.

Exercise 8.2

1. **Fill in the blanks.**
   (a) Height of a glass = 0.12 m = _____ cm
   (b) Height of a tree = 960 cm = _____ m
   (c) Height of a building = 0.1 km = _____ m
   (d) Distance from floor to ceiling = 3.8 m = _____ cm
   (e) Length of a cricket bat = 0.87 m = _____ cm
   (f) Length of a tennis racket = 72 cm = _____ mm
   (g) Height of a table = 70 cm = _____ m
   (h) Thickness of a pencil = 0.8 cm = _____ mm
   (i) Length of a mobile phone = 9.2 cm = _____ mm
   (j) Thickness of an encyclopaedia = 42 mm = _____ cm

2. **Fill in the blanks.**
   (a) 6.2 km = _____ m   (b) 0.12 km = _____ m   (c) 9.1 km = _____ m
   (d) 6300 m = _____ km   (e) 1100 m = _____ km   (f) 2800 m = _____ km

3. **Complete the table.**

	Full form	In bigger units	In smaller units
(a)	36 m 14 cm	36.14 m	3614 cm
(b)		98.98 m	9898 cm
(c)	16 m 24 cm		1624 cm
(d)	11 cm 2 mm		112 mm
(e)		2.87 cm	287 mm
(f)	49 cm 8 mm	49.8 cm	

Challenge

Three volumes of an encyclopaedia are kept on a shelf as shown. Each volume has pages that are 2 cm thick together and covers that are each 2 mm thick. If a worm starts eating from page 1 of volume 1 to the last page of volume 3, how far would it travel? (*Hint: Keep three books as shown and see where the page numbers start before giving your answer.*)

Problem Solving

(a) Mrs Kapoor has two clotheslines in her backyard. One is 5 m long and the other is 4.05 m long. How much longer is the first clothesline than the second?

(b)  A rabbit's hop is about 2 m long. How many hops does a rabbit take to travel 1 km?

(c) Varsha runs 3.2 km a day. How far does Varsha run in a week?

(d) Karan has placed a stool on a table to reach the top of his cupboard. If the height of the table is 98 cm, and the stool is 65 cm, at what height in metres is Karan standing?

(e) A bookshelf is 45 cm wide. How many books of width 9 mm can fit in the shelf?

(f)  Avinash is 1.8 m tall. Arun is 191 cm tall. How much taller is Arun than Avinash?

(g) Monika's shoe is 20.8 cm long. Kabir's shoe is 6 mm longer than Monika's shoe. How long is Kabir's shoe in cm?

Fill in the blanks.

(a) A pile of 1000 Rs 5 coins is 1500 mm high. One coin is _____ mm thick.

(b) A pile of 100 biscuits is 580 mm high. One biscuit is _____ mm thick.

(c) A pile of 10 erasers is 9.8 cm high. One eraser is _____ mm thick.

(d)  A pile of 100 comic books is 6.2 cm high. One comic book is _____ mm thick.

Project

Use a measuring tape and measure the length of the following in cm and mm. Record your findings first only in cm and then only in mm.

(a) Length of your table   (b) Length of your pencil box
(c) Thickness of your eraser   (d) Thickness of your maths text book

Measurement of Mass

You know that 1 kg = 1000 g.
Let us see how these units are related to each other using the place-value system.

	×10		×10		×10		×10		×10		×10	
Thousands kilogram kg		Hundreds hectogram		Tens decagram		Ones gram g		tenths decigram		hundredths centigram		thousandths milligram mg

÷10   ÷10   ÷10   ÷10   ÷10   ÷10

Multiply to change from a
bigger unit to a smaller one.

×1000

kg → g

÷1000

Divide to change from
a smaller unit to a bigger one.

Using Decimals to Express Mass

The weight of this puppy is 5 kg 361 g.
This can be written as 5.361 kg using
the bigger unit or 5361 g using the
smaller unit.

Converting from One Unit to Another

Apply the
SBD rule.

(a) A new born baby is 3835 g. How many
     kg is that?
     $3835 \div 1000 = 3.835$ kg

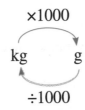

(b)

Apply the
BSM rule.

An empty suitcase is 2.50 kg. How many
g is that?
$2.50 \times 1000 = 2500$ g

Common Mistake!

5 kg 361 g
= 5.361 g ✗
= 5.361 kg ✓

1. **Fill in the blanks.**
   (a) 19.386 kg = _____ kg _____ g
   (b) 0.832 kg = _____ kg _____ g
   (c) 26 kg 14 g = _____ g
   (d) 86 kg 10 g = _____ g
   (e) 3246 g = _____ kg _____ g
   (f) 11296 g = _____ kg

2. **Find the weight in g.**

         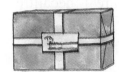

   0.42 kg   0.9 kg   1.6 kg   5.19 kg

3. **Find the weight in kg.**

   125 g   900 g   1120 g   9500 g

4. **Convert.**
   (a) 715 g = _____ kg
   (b) 0.06 kg = _____ g
   (c) 2375 g = _____ kg
   (d) 1.04 kg = _____ g
   (e) 12.1 kg = _____ g
   (f) 8008 g = _____ kg
   (g) 932 g = _____ kg
   (h) 0.35 kg = _____ g
   (i) 6125 g = _____ kg

5. (a) One egg has a mass of 50 g. How many eggs in 1 kg?

   (b)  Srinath is 1750 g heavier than his friend Kabir. If Kabir weighs 32 kg, what is Srinath's weight?

   (c) Mrs Anwar bought 500 g apples, 750 g grapes, 250 g strawberries, and 1 kg oranges. How many kg of fruit did she buy?

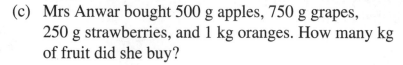

Project

A tonne is 1,000 kg. How many people together will weigh a tonne?

Record the weight of your classmates and perhaps other students also to find out how many people together weigh a tonne.

Measurement of Capacity

You know that 1 ℓ = 1000 mℓ

Let us see how these units are related to each other using the place-value system.

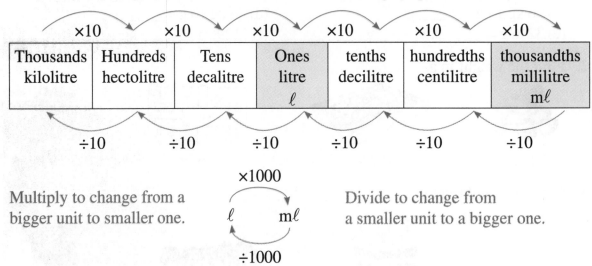

Thousands kilolitre	Hundreds hectolitre	Tens decalitre	Ones litre ℓ	tenths decilitre	hundredths centilitre	thousandths millilitre mℓ

Multiply to change from a bigger unit to smaller one.

$$\times 1000$$
$$\ell \qquad m\ell$$
$$\div 1000$$

Divide to change from a smaller unit to a bigger one.

Using Decimals to Express Capacity

This jug holds 1 ℓ 250 mℓ of lime juice. This can be written as 1.250 ℓ using the bigger unit or 1250 mℓ using the smaller unit.

Common Mistake!

1 ℓ 250 mℓ
= 1.250 mℓ ✗
= 1.250 ℓ ✓

Converting from One Unit to Another

(a) A family used 63.5 ℓ of water for bathing one day. How much is that in mℓ?
63.5 ℓ = ___?___ mℓ
63.5 × 1000 = 63500 mℓ
They used 63500 mℓ of water for bathing.

Apply the BSM rule.

(b)

16500 mℓ of water is used for cooking in one day. How much is that in ℓ?
16500 mℓ = ___?___ ℓ
16500 ÷ 1000 = 16.5 ℓ
16.5 ℓ of water is used for cooking.

Apply the SBD rule.

Exercise 8.4

1. **Match the following:**

   (a) 3 ℓ 725 mℓ   (i)   14.500 ℓ
   (b) 30 ℓ 725 mℓ   (ii) 8685 mℓ
   (c) 8.685 ℓ   (iii) 30.725 ℓ
   (d) 80685 mℓ   (iv) 3725 mℓ
   (e) 1.450 ℓ   (v)   80.685 ℓ
   (f) 14500 mℓ   (vi) 1 ℓ 450 mℓ

2. **Find the capacity in mℓ.**

   1.3 ℓ   15.5 ℓ   0.35 ℓ   0.9 ℓ

3. **Find the capacity in ℓ.**

   335 mℓ   950 mℓ   2500 mℓ   5250 mℓ

4. **Convert the following.**

   (a) 0.4 ℓ = _____ mℓ   (b) 8.03 ℓ = _____ mℓ   (c) 0.14 ℓ = _____ mℓ
   (d) 750 mℓ = _____ ℓ   (e) 15.35 ℓ = _____ mℓ   (f) 100 mℓ = _____ ℓ
   (g) 4000 mℓ = _____ ℓ   (h) 1840 mℓ = _____ ℓ   (i) 1.25 ℓ = _____ mℓ

5. **Problem solving.**

   (a) A bottle of juice holds 750 mℓ of juice. Can two such bottles be poured into a jar that holds 1.5 ℓ?

   (b) A kettle holds about 900 mℓ of tea. How many tea cups of 150 mℓ each can it fill? (**Hint:** *Use repeated subtraction.*)

   (c) A shower drips at the rate of 150 mℓ an hour. How many litres of water would drip from it in 8 hours?

Project

Calculate the amount of water a tap, that has not been shut properly, loses in a minute, an hour, a day, a week, a month, and a year. Put up the information on a bulletin board and encourage people to save water. (First collect the amount of water that drips in a minute and measure with a measuring glass. Use this measurement to calculate the rest.)

Theme: A School Play!

(a) A cardboard door was made for the school play by sticking 2 sheets of cardboard, one 5 mm thick and the other 7 mm thick. How thick was the door?

5 mm + 7 mm = _____ mm

12 mm = _____ cm _____ mm

The door was _____ cm _____ mm thick.

(b) The teacher draws a line 3 m 75 cm long on the floor of stage to guide the dancers. Later she increased the length by another 2 m 50 cm. How long is the line now?

3 m 75 cm + 2 m 50 cm = ?

3 m + 2 m = _____ m

75 cm + 50 cm = _____ cm

125 cm = _____ m _____ cm

5 m + 1 m 25 cm = _____ m _____ cm

The line is _____ m _____ cm long now.

(c) There were two earthenware pots kept on the stage. One weighed 980 g and the other weighed 1 kg 200 g. How heavy were both the pots together?

1 kg 200 g + 980 g = ?

1 kg 200 g + 980 g = 1 kg 1180 g

But 1180 g = 1 kg 180 g

So 1 kg + 1 kg 180 g = 2 kg 180 g

Both pots together weigh 2 kg 180 g.

(d) For one scene 13 ℓ 500 mℓ water was poured into a bucket of 24 ℓ capacity. How much more water could the bucket hold?

24 ℓ – 13 ℓ 500 mℓ = ?

24 ℓ is the same as 23 ℓ 1000 mℓ

23 ℓ – 13 ℓ = 10 ℓ

1000 mℓ – 500 mℓ = 500 mℓ

There was space enough for 10 ℓ 500 mℓ more water in the bucket.

(e) Out of 2 kg of sweets that was kept for distribution to all the actors after the play, 250 g was still remaining. How much was eaten?

2 kg – 250 g = ?

2 kg is the same as 1 kg 1000 g.

1 kg 1000 g – 250 g = 1 kg 750 g

1 kg 750 g was eaten.

 **Exercise 8.5**

1. **Add.**
    (a) 17 m + 12 m 6 cm
    (b) 6 cm 5 mm + 1 cm 9 mm
    (c) 5 kg 200 g + 6 kg 800 g
    (d) 1 kg 500 g + 1 kg 750 g
    (e) 2 ℓ 250 mℓ + 900 mℓ
    (f) 5 ℓ 600 mℓ + 2 ℓ 500 mℓ

2. **Subtract.**
    (a) 10 m – 6 m 50 cm
    (b) 7 cm 8 mm – 1 cm 9 mm
    (c) 2 kg 200 g – 1 kg 100 g
    (d) 5 kg – 1 kg 250 g
    (e) 2 ℓ 800 mℓ – 1 ℓ 100 mℓ
    (f) 10 ℓ 250 mℓ – 1 ℓ 750 mℓ

3. **Application in real life.**
    (a) A snail travelled 2 m 32 cm on one day and 1 m 93 cm on the second day. How far had the snail travelled in all?

    (b) A worm climbing up a high wall went 12 m on one day but slipped back by 2 m 35 cm in the evening. How far up had the worm reached on that day?

    (c) 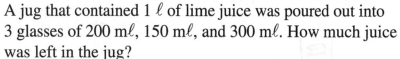 A jug that contained 1 ℓ of lime juice was poured out into 3 glasses of 200 mℓ, 150 mℓ, and 300 mℓ. How much juice was left in the jug?

    (d) A gold brick weighing 4 kg was melted. It lost 150 g of weight during melting. How much gold was left in the brick?

    (e) A porter was carrying two bags—one weighing 16 kg 800 g and the other weighing 10 kg 950 g. How much weight was the porter carrying?

Project

Take the help of a teacher to use the science laboratory in your school. Find the weight of these.

Calculate to find these answers.

5-rupee coin = _____ g   (a) Find the weight of 100 Rs 2 coins.
2-rupee coin = _____ g   (b) What will be the weight of 1000 Re 1 coins?
1-rupee coin = _____ g   (c) How many Rs 5 coins in 900 g?

Estimating Measures

Anju is having a birthday party. She has invited 15 friends over. She thinks 3 litres of juice should be enough to serve 15 people. She decorates the room with streamers. She buys ten 5 metre strips for decoration.

Anju has used **estimation**. She mentally measures the juice and streamers to decide whether they will be enough.

In real life, we often estimate measures. But before we estimate we need to have experience of real measures.

The following illustrations may help you.

About 1 mg

About 1 g

About 1 kg

Comparison helps in estimation. My finger is about 1 cm wide. The pencil is about 12 finger widths, so the pencil is about 12 cm.

About 1 mℓ

About 1 ℓ

Thickness of a finger nail
About 1 mm

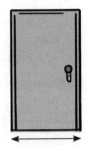

Width of an index finger
About 1 cm

Breadth of a door
About 1 m

Try This

Fill in the blanks.
(a) A slice of bread weighs about 24 _____.
(b) A dropper for medicine holds 2 _____.
(c) A bench is about 2 _____ long.

Exercise 8.6

1. Circle the correct answer.

(a)
9 g/500 g

(b)
750 g/100 g

(c)
500 g/500 kg

(d)
120 kg/120 g

(e)
3 ℓ/30 ℓ

(f)
1 ℓ/10 ℓ

(g)
100 g/100 kg

(h)
300 mℓ/30 mℓ

(i)
length of a chalk
8 cm/80 cm

(j)
length of shoe laces
500 cm/50 cm

(k)
length of an aeroplane
900 m/70 m

(l)
thickness of
a needle
2 mm/10 mm

2. Fill in the blanks with the correct unit.

(a) A bicycle weighs about 25 _____.

(b) A bottle of sauce has 500 _____ of sauce.

(c) A car is about 3 _____ long.

(d) A bucket holds about 20 _____ of water.

(e) The length of a latch is about 12 _____.

(f) A bottle of an aerated drink holds about 300 _____.

> First decide whether you need a unit of length, capacity, or mass. Then choose the correct one.

3. Estimate in cm. Then measure to check the estimate.

	Estimate (in cm)	Actual (in cm)	Difference (in cm)
(a) Length of your pencil			
(b) Length of your thumb			
(c) Length of your eraser			
(d) Length of your book			
(e) Length of your table			

CHAPTER CHECK-UP

1. **Convert.**
   (a) 0.8 km = _____ m
   (b) 1500 m = _____ km
   (c) 8.4 km = _____ m
   (d) 0.18 m = _____ cm
   (e) 720 cm = _____ m
   (f) 3.5 m = _____ cm
   (g) 1.2 cm = _____ mm
   (h) 220 mm = _____ cm
   (i) 0.3 cm = _____ mm

2. (a) 850 g = _____ kg
   (b) 0.09 kg = _____ g
   (c) 1380 g = _____ kg
   (d) 0.90 kg = _____ g
   (e) 1.15 kg = _____ g
   (f) 2200 g = _____ kg

3. (a) 0.5 ℓ = _____ mℓ
   (b) 0.17 ℓ = _____ mℓ
   (c) 1880 mℓ = _____ ℓ
   (d) 7.25 ℓ = _____ mℓ
   (e) 200 mℓ = _____ ℓ
   (f) 950 mℓ = _____ ℓ

4. **Cross out the wrong one.**
   (a) A book weighs about 20 g/200 g.

   (b) A bottle of medicine has 50 mℓ/5000 mℓ of liquid.

   (c) A pencil is about 15 cm/150 cm long.

5. **Measure the length of these insects.**

   (a) Grasshopper

   (b) Ladybird

6. (a) Mrs Arora buys 1 m 40 cm of cloth for her younger son and 1 m 80 cm of cloth for her older son. How much cloth does she buy in all?

   (b) A full suitcase weighs 9 kg 100g. A book weighing 750 g was removed from it. What is the weight of the suitcase now?

   (c) 1 ℓ 200 mℓ oil was used up from an oil can of 5 ℓ. How much is left in the can now?

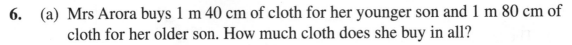

LOOKING BEYOND

Enrichment Time

Speed, Distance, and Time

You must have often seen lightning in the sky before you heard the thunder. That is because the speed of light is much faster than the speed of sound.

Light travels at 3,00,000 km per second and sound travels at 343 metres per second.

Speed is calculated by dividing the distance travelled by the time it takes to travel that distance.

In everyday life, we need to calculate the speed of cars, trains, planes, or even a person walking. If a car goes 340 km in 4 hours, its speed is:

340 ÷ 4 = **85 km per hour** (kmph)

Answer these questions.

1. I have gone 350 km in 5 hours. What is my speed?

2. I have walked 6 km in 2 hours. What is my speed?

3. I have flown 7560 km in 7 hours. What is my speed?

4. I have gone 720 km in 6 hours. What is my speed?

5. I fly 120 km in 4 hours. What is my speed?

6. I hopped 45 km in 3 hours. What is my speed?

Area and Perimeter

Looking Back

Perimeter is the distance around the edge of a figure.

The perimeter of this stamp is
3 cm + 4 cm + 3 cm + 4 cm = 14 cm.

Area is the amount of surface a figure covers.

The stamp covers 12 squares of 1 cm sides. The area of this stamp is 12 square centimetres or 12 sq. cm.

1. **Find the perimeter of these posters.**

35 cm

35 cm

60 cm

24 cm

50 cm

50 cm

2. **Find the area of these stickers. Give your answers in sq. units.**

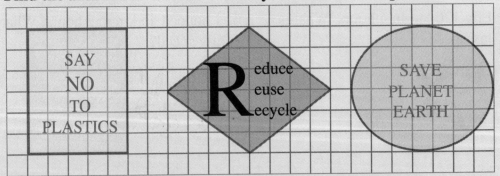

SAY
NO
TO
PLASTICS

Reduce
Reuse
Recycle

SAVE
PLANET
EARTH

3. Use a cm squared sheet of paper. Draw the outline of your hand on it. Find the perimeter and the area of your hand.

Perimeter of a Rectangle

Asmi has designed a flag for her school sports team.

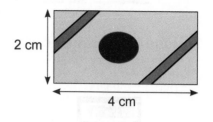

The perimeter of Asmi's flag is:
4 cm + 2 cm + 4 cm + 2 cm = 12 cm

Since we are adding 2 lengths and 2 breadths of equal size, we can also find the perimeter by using a shortcut.

Perimeter of a rectangle = 2 × (length + breadth)

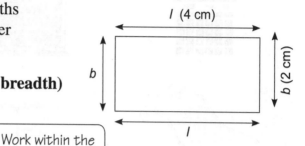

$P = 2 (l + b)$
Here l = 4 cm; b = 2 cm
$P = 2 (4 + 2)$
$= 2 × 6 = 12$ cm
Perimeter of the flag = 12 cm

Work within the bracket first.

Perimeter of a Square

Asmi's sister has drawn this picture of her favourite cartoon character. Find its perimeter.

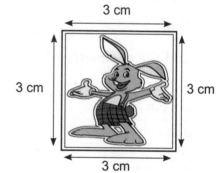

The perimeter of this picture is:
3 cm + 3 cm + 3 cm + 3 cm = 12 cm

All the sides of a square are equal.
So perimeter = side + side + side + side

Perimeter of a square = 4 × length of side

This is a shortcut!

$P = 4 × 3$
$P = 12$ cm
Perimeter of the picture = 12 cm

Try This

Find the perimeter of the following.

(a)   14 cm

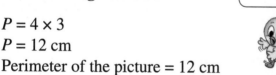

14 cm

(b)   11 cm

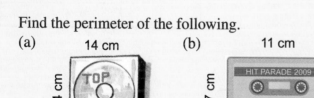

7 cm

Always remember to mention the units in your answer.

1. **Find the perimeter of these objects by using the shortcut.**

(a) 30 cm
90 cm

(b) 153 cm
122 cm

(c) 92 cm
80 cm

(d) 50 cm
30 cm

(e) 70 cm
90 cm

(f) 60 cm
60 cm

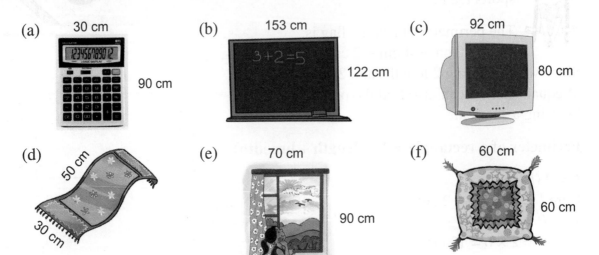

2. **Find the perimeter of these squares.**

	(a)	(b)	(c)	(d)	(e)	(f)	(g)	(h)	(i)	(j)
Side of square in cm	3	5	11	18	25	30	41	55	63	92
Perimeter in cm	12									

(**Hint:** $4 \times 3 = 12$)

3. **Find the perimeter of these rectangles.**

	(a)	(b)	(c)	(d)	(e)	(f)	(g)	(h)	(i)	(j)
l in cm	2	2	3	5	5	3	4	5	8	7
b in cm	3	4	4	4	2	6	6	6	6	9
P in cm	10									

(**Hint:** $2 + 3 = 5; 2 \times 5 = 10$)

4. **The perimeter is given. Find the side of these squares.**

	(a)	(b)	(c)	(d)	(e)	(f)	(g)	(h)	(i)	(j)
P in cm	28	40	64	96	120	172	232	300	384	556
Side of square in cm	7									

(**Hint:** $28 \div 4 = 7$)

Exploring Perimeter

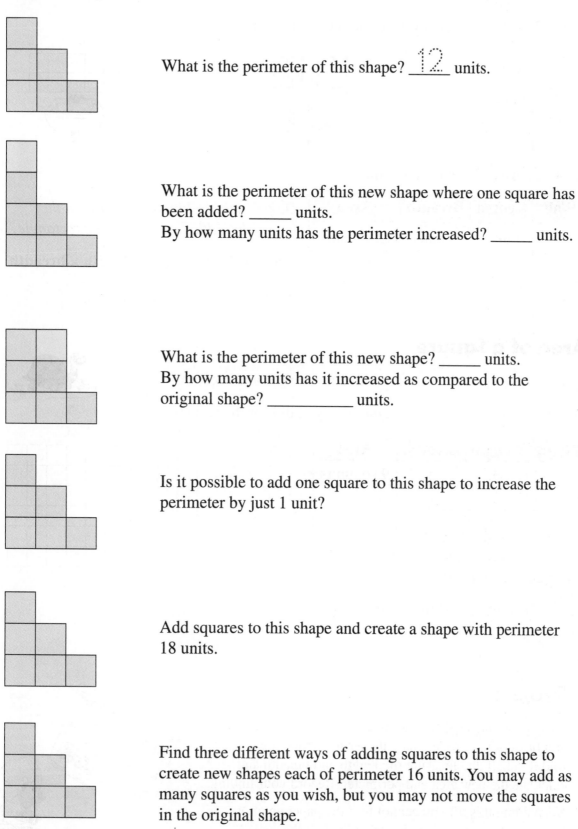

What is the perimeter of this shape? __12__ units.

What is the perimeter of this new shape where one square has been added? _____ units.
By how many units has the perimeter increased? _____ units.

What is the perimeter of this new shape? _____ units.
By how many units has it increased as compared to the original shape? _____ units.

Is it possible to add one square to this shape to increase the perimeter by just 1 unit?

Add squares to this shape and create a shape with perimeter 18 units.

Find three different ways of adding squares to this shape to create new shapes each of perimeter 16 units. You may add as many squares as you wish, but you may not move the squares in the original shape.

Area of a Rectangle

The wall in front of each washbasin has been tiled.

A

B

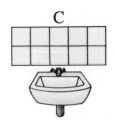

C

Find the area of each tiled wall.

Wall	Length	Breadth	Area
A	4 units	3 units	12 sq. units
B			
C			

Do you see a relationship between the length, breadth, and area of the rectangle?

Area of the rectangle = length × breadth

$A = l \times b$

This is a shortcut!

Area of a Square

A square is a special rectangle with equal length and breadth.

Fill in the columns for these squares as you did for the rectangles.

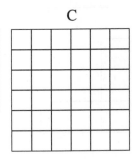

A   B   C

Figure	Length	Breadth	Area
A	3	3	9 sq. units
B			
C			

Do you see a relationship between the length, breadth, and area of a square?

Area of a square = Side × Side

$A = S \times S$

Project

Take a newspaper sheet and measure and record its length and breadth in cm. Calculate its perimeter and area. Then fold it in half and measure the length and breadth and calculate the new area and perimeter. Record your findings.

Keep doing this till you cannot fold the paper anymore. Compare you findings with a friend's. Is it the same?

Exercise 9.2

1. Use the shortcut to find the area of these figures. Give your answer in square units.

   (a)

   $l =$ _____ ; $b =$ _____
   $A =$ _____

   (b)

   $l =$ _____ ; $b =$ _____
   $A =$ _____

   (c)

   $l =$ _____ ; $b =$ _____
   $A =$ _____

2. Find the area of these shapes using the shortcut. Give your answer in square units.

   (a)

   (b)

   (c)

3. Use a cm ruler to find the length and breadth of these shapes. Then find their area using the shortcut. Give your answer in sq. cm.

   (a)

   (b)

   (c)

4. Find the area of these paintings. Give your answer in sq. cm.

   (a)

   (b)

5. Find the area of these shapes.

   (a) $l = 9$ cm $b = 5$ cm
   (b) $l = 12$ cm $b = 10$ cm
   (c) $l = 13$ cm $b = 5$ cm
   (d) $l = 15$ cm $b = 1.5$ cm
   (e) $l = 9$ cm $b = 2.1$ cm
   (f) $l = 10$ cm $b = 5.2$ cm

6. Fill in the columns.

	(a)	(b)	(c)	(d)	(e)	(f)	(g)	(h)	(i)	(j)
Length in cm	7	4	2	9			13	11		
Breadth in cm	3				7	4			20	8
Area in sq. cm	21	48	16	36	42	112	130	187	220	136

Area of a Triangle

Ragini has cut a rectangle out of cm squared paper like this.

What is the area of the rectangle? _____ sq. cm.

She then cuts the rectangle into two equal triangles like this.
What is the area of each triangle?

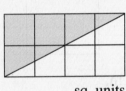

Since triangle A is half the rectangle, its area will be half the area of the rectangle.

So, the area of triangle A = 3 sq. cm.

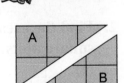
Give the area of the shaded triangle in each figure.

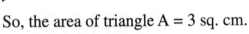

_____ sq. units   _____ sq. units   _____ sq. units

Challenge

Find the area of these shapes.

Break it up into rectangles and triangles.

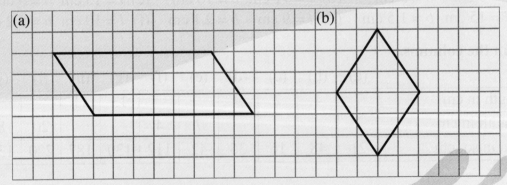

(a)

(b)

Next Ragini cut another rectangle like this. Its area is 20 sq. units.

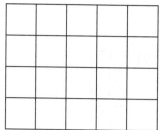

If she cuts a triangle out of it like this, what will its area be?

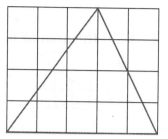

To find the area of the triangle, we can look at the big rectangle as two smaller rectangles like this. Then let us look at each small rectangle separately.

A   B

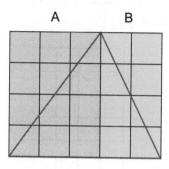

A

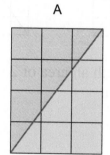

Rectangle A = 12 sq. units
Triangle A = 6 sq. units

B

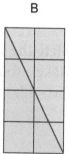

Rectangle B = 8 sq. units
Triangle B = 4 sq. units

Looking at it together

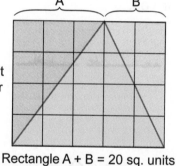

Rectangle A + B = 20 sq. units
Triangle A + B = 10 sq. units

Try This

First find the area of the rectangle. Then break it up into smaller rectangles to find the area of the triangles.

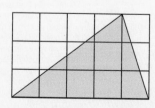

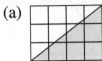  **Exercise 9.3**

1. Find the area of these triangles.

(a)   (b)   (c) 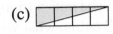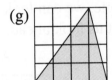 (d)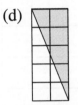

(e) 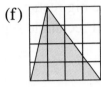 (f)  (g) (h)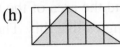

3. Complete the shapes.

(a) Make a four-sided figure with an area of 2 sq. cm. Two sides are drawn for you.

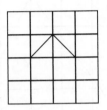

(b) Make a four-sided figure with an area of 8 sq. cm. Two sides are drawn for you.

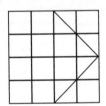

 Challenge

Draw 2 more sides to the shape given here. Find three ways to make four-sided shapes with an area of 10 sq. cm. One is done for you.

 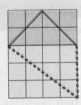 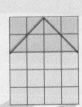

Different Units of Area

Area is always measured in square units. The unit we choose depends on how large or small the area being measured is.

A square with 1 cm sides is a square centimetre (sq. cm).

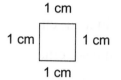

 A fingernail is about 1 sq. cm.

A square with 1 metre sides is a square metre (sq. m).

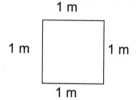

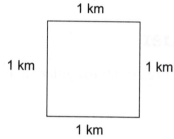 A single bedsheet is about 2 sq. m.

A square with 1 kilometre sides is a square kilometre (sq. km).

The state of Tripura has an area of about 10,500 sq. km.

Smaller areas are measured in sq. cm and large areas in sq. km.

A sq. km. is a very large unit of area. Your school playground is perhaps smaller than 1 sq. km.

Try This

Say which unit you would prefer to use to find the area of these—sq. cm, sq. m., or sq. km.

(a) Label
(b) A very large lake
(c) Swimming pool
(d) Strip of tablets
(e) TV screen
(f) Lakshwadeep Islands
(g) Blackboard
(h) Cricket field
(i) Cushion cover
(j) City of Bhopal

Project

Rajasthan is the largest state in India with an area of 3,42,239 sq. km. There are about 165 people living in a sq. km. Find out the area of your state and how many people live in a sq. km.

Draw a 1 cm by 1 cm square on a paper and cut it out. Then, make a square metre out of newspaper using cello tape. Now try to answer these.

	Guess	Actual
Number of times you can write 'a' in a sq. cm.	_____	_____
Number of rice grains that can fit in a sq. cm.	_____	_____
Number of Enjoying Mathematics books that can fit in a sq. m.	_____	_____
Number of people that can stand in a sq. m.	_____	_____
Number of people that can sit in a sq. m.	_____	_____
Area of your classroom in sq. m.	_____	_____
Area of any one wall in your classroom in sq. m.	_____	_____

Area of Irregular Shapes

You remember that we found the area of an irregular shape in Class IV using this method.
There are 5 whole squares.
The are 12 partial squares which may be estimated as 8 squares.
Approximate area = 5 + 8 = about 13 square units.

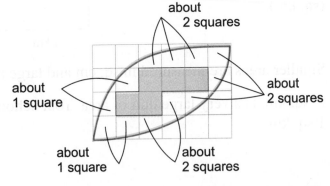
about 2 squares
about 2 squares
about 1 square
about 1 square
about 2 squares

You can also estimate the area of an irregular figure using a shortcut.

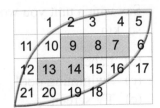

- Find the **under estimate** by counting only the whole squares. There are 5 whole squares.
- Find the **over estimate** by counting all the squares (whole and part). There are 21 such squares.
- **Add** the two figures and divide by 2 (ignore the remainder if any).
  5 + 21 = 26
  26 ÷ 2 = 13
  Approximate area = 13 square units

The answers in both the methods are same in this example. It is also possible that the answers can be close, but not necessarily the same, as both are approximate or estimated answers.

Exercise 9.4

1. **Estimate the area of each of these figures in square units.**

(a)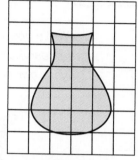

(b)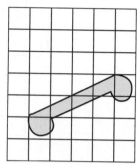

(c)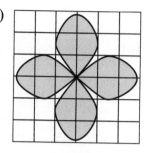

(d)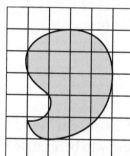

(e)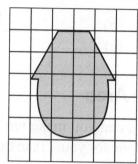

(f)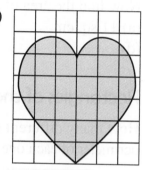

2. **Find the approximate area of these islands. Take each square centimetre in the drawing to be the same as one sq. km. Give your answers in sq. km.**

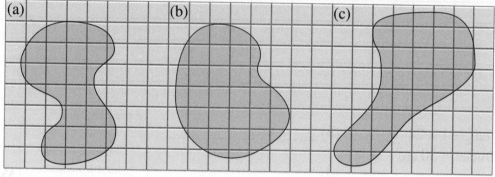

Refer Maths Lab Activity on Page 171

Relationship between Area and Perimeter

Rectangles of the Same Perimeter

How many different kinds of rectangles can you make with a perimeter of 24 cm? (Take the squares below to be 1 cm × 1 cm.)

(a)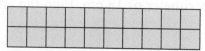

(b)

(c)

(d)

(e)

(f)

> Write down your observation in your own words.

Now find the area of each one.

(a) 11 sq. cm

(b) _____

(c) _____

(d) _____

(e) _____

(f) _____

Rectangles of the Same Area

How many different rectangles can you make with an area of 24 sq. cm? Find the perimeter of each one. One is done for you. (Take the squares below to be 1 cm × 1 cm.)

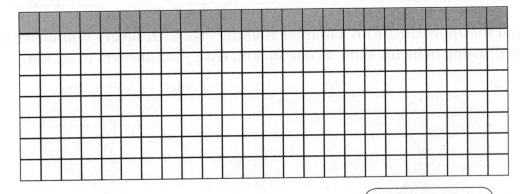

(a) Rectangle 1 × 24
   Perimeter = 50 cm

(b) _____

(c) _____

(d) _____

> Write down your observation in your own words.

Exercise 9.5

1. Use a 15-cm-long string and join its ends. Place it on a centimetre squared paper to make a square, a circle, a triangle, and a rectangle. Find the area of each shape. Which shape has the largest area? Which shape has the smallest area?

2. Use a centimetre squared paper to create as many different rectangles as you can with a perimeter of 18 cm. Find the area of each rectangle.

3. Use centimetre squared paper to create as many different rectangles as you can with an area of 36 sq. cm. Find the perimeter of each rectangle.

4. **A pentomino is a figure made up of 5 equal squares joined together to share sides.**
   (a) These are two examples of pentominoes.

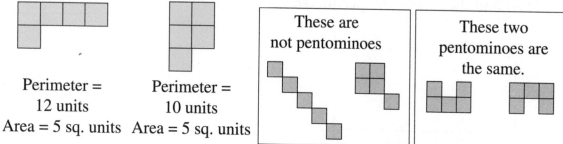

Perimeter =
12 units

Perimeter =
10 units

Area = 5 sq. units   Area = 5 sq. units

These are
not pentominoes

These two
pentominoes are
the same.

It is possible to make 12 different kinds of pentominoes. Explore on a cm squared paper to find all of them.

   (b) Once you have found all the 12 pentominoes, stick them on card paper, cut them out, and use them like jigsaw pieces. Try to find a way to fit all the 12 pieces to create a large rectangle.

5. **Application in real life.**
   (a) The breadth of a garden is 9.3 m and its length is 17.7 m. What is the perimeter of the garden?

   (b) Prabhu has a rectangular backyard that is 32 m wide and 46 m long. How much fencing will he need to enclose the yard? If fencing costs Rs 98 per metre, how much will he have to pay?

   (c) Sapna walks around a square park whose side is 70 m. One day she walked around the park 5 times. How much did she walk in all?

   (d) A square picture has a frame of 100 cm. What is the length of each side?

   (e) A square field has a perimeter of 360 m. What is its area?

   (f) 150 cm of lace was used to edge a pillow. If the width of the pillow was 25 cm, what is its length?

   (g) How many square tiles of sides 10 cm will be needed to tile a floor which is 300 cm long and 500 cm wide? (*Hint: First find the area of the floor and then divide by the area of each tile.*)

CHAPTER CHECK-UP

1. Use your centimetre ruler to find the length and breadth of these shapes.
   Then find their area and perimeter.

   (a)

   (b)

2. Find the perimeter and area of:
   (a) a square with sides 7 cm.
   (b) a rectangle with length 5 m and breadth 11 m.

3. Find the area of these shapes in square units.

   (a) 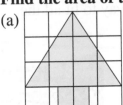   (b) 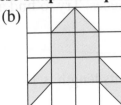   (c) 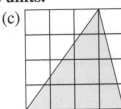   (d)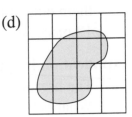

4. Which unit will you use to measure these areas—sq. cm, sq. m, or sq. km?
   (a) a mobile phone   (b) the base of a glass   (c) a large curtain
   (d) the area of a zoo   (e) the area of Baroda   (f) the area of a watch dial

5. How many rectangles can you make with a perimeter of 12 sq. cm? Find the area of each.

6. (a) A playground has length 230 m and breadth 415 m. What is the perimeter of the playground?

   (b) Find the length of a room whose area is 96 sq. m and breadth is 6 m.

   (c) A carpet is 10 m long and 7 m wide. What are its area and perimeter?

   (d) Find the length of the side of a square stamp with an area of 4 sq. cm.

MATHS LAB ACTIVITY

Objective: To create a tessellating pattern.

Materials Required: Plain paper, a pair of scissors, card paper, cello tape, pencil, crayons.

Preparation: Card paper may be cut into a 6 cm × 6 cm square.

M. C. Escher was a well-known Dutch artist who used tessellation to create beautiful designs.

Steps:

1. Take the square card paper.

2. Mark out a portion as shown.

3. Cut it and attach it to the opposite side without overlapping and by using cello tape.

4. Now mark out another portion as shown.

5. Cut and attach to the opposite side.

6. Your basic stencil is ready. Use it to draw repeated shapes like this. Then fill in details to make an interesting design.

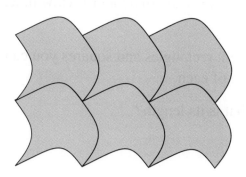

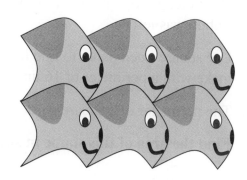

Experiment with different cut out portions to create other interesting designs.

TEST YOUR SKILLS*

1. **Which of these are lines of symmetry?**

2. **Write $\frac{1}{2}$, $\frac{1}{4}$, $\frac{1}{3}$, or $\frac{1}{6}$ turn next to each shape to show the turn it needs to come back to its original shape.**

3. **Complete the pattern till it comes back to its original position.**

4. **If 250 g more cotton is stuffed into a pillow that already has 850 g cotton in it, what will be the weight of the pillow?**

5. **Out of length of 3 m 50 cm of ribbon, 1 m 75 cm was used to tie a gift. How much ribbon was left?**

6. **Use square lined paper to find how many different rectangles and squares you can make with a perimeter of 16 units. Find the area of each.**

7. **The perimeter of a square garden is 908 m. What is its length?**

8. **Find the area of this shape in square units.**

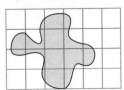

* This is for Chapters 7, 8, and 9.

Volume and Nets

Volume

The twins Shweta and Swati were comparing the size of their snack boxes. Shweta's box was a little longer while Swati's box seemed a little higher. But they could not decide whose box was bigger.

Their mother cut their sandwiches into small square pieces and told them to find out how many they could fit in each of their boxes.

Shweta put one layer of 8 pieces.

1 layer

Swati could fit only 6 pieces in one layer in her box.

1 layer

Then she put one more layer of 8 pieces. There was no more space left in her snack box.

2 layers

She could fit two more such layers in the box. Then the box was full.

3 layers

Shweta's box could hold (8 × 2) = 16 sandwich pieces.
Swati's box cold hold (6 × 3) = 18 sandwich pieces.
So, we can say that Swati's snack box is bigger because it could hold more pieces.
We can say that Swati's snack box has a greater **'volume'** than Shweta's snack box.
The volume of an object is the amount of space it occupies.

In order to find the volume of objects we fill them up with cubes. We can choose one of the three kinds:

1 mm

1 mm

A millimetre cube (mm cube) is about the size of a grain of sugar.

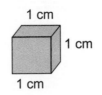

1 cm

1 cm

1 cm

A centimetre cube (cm cube) is about the size of a die.

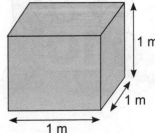

1 m

1 m

1 m

A metre cube (m cube) is about the size of a very large TV box.

A mm cube is used to measure the volume of very small objects.
A m cube is used to measure the volume of large objects.

Let us find the volume of this shoe box by filling it with cm cubes.

Put in 1 cm cubes to fit one layer and count them. There are 10 rows with 4 cubes in each row. So there are 40 cubes in one layer. There are four layers of 40 cubes each. There are 160 one-cm cubes filling the box.

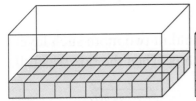

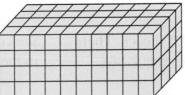

> Whether a box is full or empty it takes up the same amount of space on your shelf. So both have the same volume.

Since the box can hold 160 one-cm cubes, the **volume of the box is said to be 160 cubic centimetres**.

The unit of measurement of volume is cubic centimetres and is written as cu. cm.
Volume of the shoe box = 160 cu. cm

1 mm cubes give the volume in cubic millimetres and is written as cu. mm.

1 m cubes give the volume in cubic metres and is written as cu. m.

Find the volume of this solid.

(a)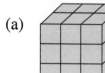
One layer = 3 × 2 = 6 cubes
   3 layers = 6 × 3 = 18 cubes
      Volume = 18 cu. cm.

(b)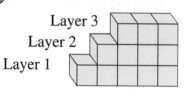

Layer 3
Layer 2
Layer 1

Add the different layers.

Layer 1   5
Layer 2   4
Layer 3   3
            ——
            12
            ——

Answer: Volume = 12 cu. cm

 Exercise 10.1

1. **Find the volume of each of these cuboids. Give your answer in cu. cm.**

(a)   (b)   (c)    (d)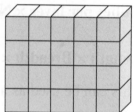

(e)    (f)   (g)   (h)

2. **Find the volume of each of these solid shapes. Give your answer in cu. cm.**

(a) 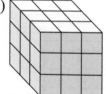   (b)   (c) 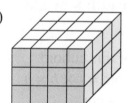   (d)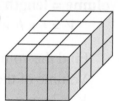

(e) 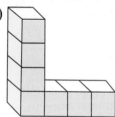   (f) 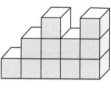 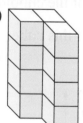   (g) 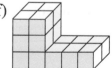   (h)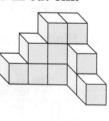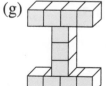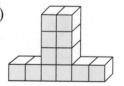

Challenge

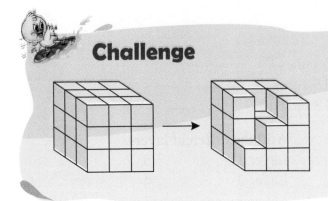

What is the total volume of the cubes that have been removed from the first figure to make the second figure? Take each to be a cm. cube.

Calculating Volume

We can use a shortcut to calculate the volume of a cuboid. While finding the volume of a cube or a cuboid, you have been first counting the number of cubes in a layer and then finding the number of layers.

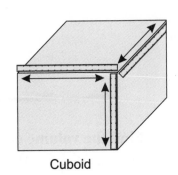

Cuboid

Cubes per layer × Number of layers = Volume

Length × Breadth × Height = Volume

This can be used as a shortcut to calculate the volume.

Volume = length × breadth × height

$$V = \ell \times b \times h$$

(a) Find the volume of this cuboid.
Volume of the cuboid = $\ell \times b \times h$
$V = 7 \text{ cm} \times 4 \text{ cm} \times 4 \text{ cm}$
$V = 112 \text{ cu. cm}$
Answer: Volume of the cuboid is 112 cu. cm.

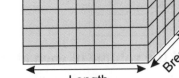

Height
4 cm

Breadth
4 cm

Length
7 cm

(b) Find the volume of this cube.

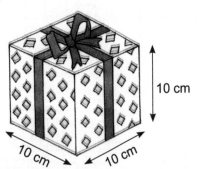

10 cm

10 cm   10 cm

Volume of a cube = $\ell \times b \times h$
$V = 10 \text{ cm} \times 10 \text{ cm} \times 10 \text{ cm}$
$V = 10 \times 10 \times 10 \text{ cu. cm}$
$V = 1{,}000 \text{ cu. cm}$
Answer: Volume of the cube is 1,000 cu. cm.

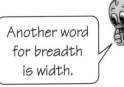

Another word for breadth is width.

Try This

$\ell = 40 \text{ cm}$ $b = 1 \text{ cm}$ $h = 60 \text{ cm}$
$V = ?$

Exercise 10.2

1. Use a ruler to measure the length, breadth, and height of these objects to the nearest cm. Then calculate their volume.

Your Maths text book
ℓ _____ cm b _____ cm h _____ cm
Volume = _____ cu. cm

Your eraser
ℓ _____ cm b _____ cm h _____ cm
Volume = _____ cu. cm

Your pencil box
ℓ _____ cm b _____ cm h _____ cm
Volume = _____ cu. cm

Your desk top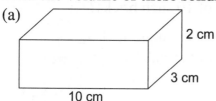
ℓ _____ cm b _____ cm h _____ cm
Volume = _____ cu. cm

2. **Find the volume of these solids.**

(a)
10 cm, 3 cm, 2 cm

(b)
5 cm, 3 cm, 4 cm

(c)
12 mm, 4 mm, 8 mm

3. **Find the volume of these objects.**

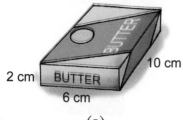
(a)
2 cm, BUTTER, 6 cm, 10 cm

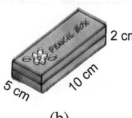
(b)
PENCIL BOX, 2 cm, 5 cm, 10 cm

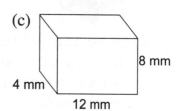
(c)
8 cm, CRAYONS, 12 cm, 3 cm

(d)
4 cm, 6 cm, 5 cm

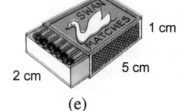
(e)
SWAN MATCHES, 1 cm, 2 cm, 5 cm

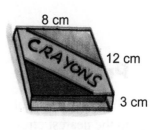
(f)
3 cm, 2 cm, 15 cm

4. **Find the volume of each of the following.**

   (a) $\ell = 12$ mm
   $b = 20$ mm
   $h = 13$ mm
   $V =$ _____ cu. mm

   (b) $\ell = 15$ cm
   $b = 9$ cm
   $h = 11$ cm
   $V =$ _____ cu. cm

   (c) $\ell = 8$ m
   $b = 3$ m
   $h = 16$ m
   $V =$ _____ cu. m

5. **Complete the table.**

	Length	Breadth	Height	Volume
(a)	3 m	8 m	7 m	
(b)	6 cm	4 cm		120 cu. cm
(c)	14 cm		8 cm	448 cu. cm
(d)		11 mm	10 mm	1210 cu. mm
(e)	3 m	4 m	9 m	

Hint: Divide 120 by the product of 6 and 4 to get the height.

6. **Application in real life.**

   (a) A book is 24 cm long, 14 cm wide, and 2 cm high. What is the volume of 2 such books piled one on top of the other?

   (b) The drawer in Kalpana's cupboard is 30 cm long, 10 cm high, and 45 cm wide. What is the volume of the drawer?

   (c) 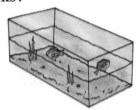 A brick has a length of 18 cm, breadth of 6 cm, and height of 5 cm. What will be the volume of 10 such bricks?

   (d) A fish tank is 40 cm long, 60 cm wide, and 50 cm high. It has been half filled with water. What volume of the tank has not been filled? (**Hint:** *Take half the height of the tank to find the volume.*)

Project

Find the volume of a matchbox by measuring the sides to the nearest cm.
What do you think will be the volume of a tower that is 2 matchboxes high?
Build a tower using 20 matchboxes such that it is 5 matchboxes high (see illustration). What is the volume of this tower?
Now use the same matchboxes to build a tower that is 10 matchboxes high. What is its volume?
What do you observe?

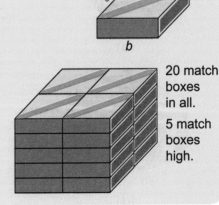

20 match boxes in all.

5 match boxes high.

Nets

Ashima has an empty matchbox.

She opens the outer cover carefully.

She then opens the inside box.

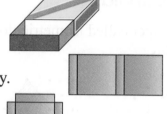

All six faces of a cube are identical squares.

The opened shapes are called nets. How many rectangles on each of these nets?

This is the net of a cube.

  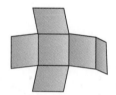 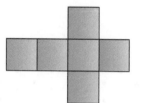

This net has _____ squares.
This net can also be folded back to make a cube.

Try This

Cut out a square piece of card paper with sides of 10 cm. Copy the net below by outlining the square six times as shown. The sides should touch.
Cut out the whole shape.

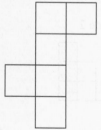

Fold along the dotted lines. Seal the cube with the help of a cello tape.

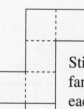

Stick pictures of your family and friends on each side.

Challenge

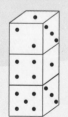

What is the total of all the sides of the dice that are touching each other plus the one on top and bottom?

Hint: The opposite sides of a dice add up to 7.

Drawing Cubes and Cuboids

You can use special dotted paper called isometric dot paper to help you draw solid shapes like cubes and cuboids.

Normal
dotted paper

Isometric
dot paper
held correctly

Isometric
dot paper
held incorrectly

The shaded shape on the isometric dots tells you which way the paper should be held.

Try This

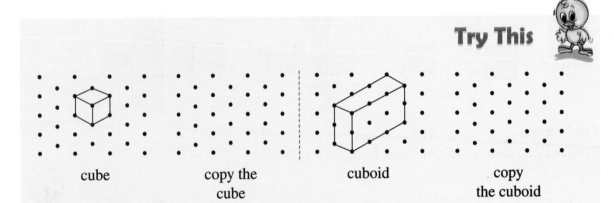

cube   copy the cube   cuboid   copy the cuboid

Shapes often look different when you view them from different directions.

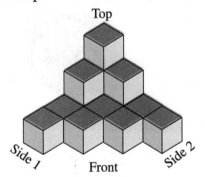

Top

Side 1   Front   Side 2

The picture on the left gives the front view of the shape. The pictures below show the other views.

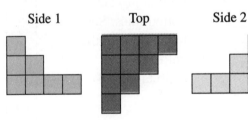

Side 1   Top   Side 2

Try This

Colour to match the view of each shape.

Top   Side 1   Side 2

1. Which of these nets can be folded to make cubes?

(a) 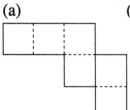 (b) 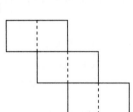 (c) 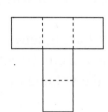 (d)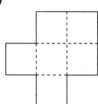

2. Complete the following figures to make cuboids.

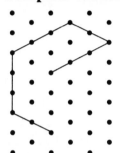 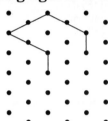 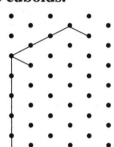 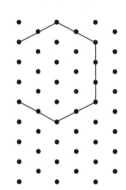

3. Match the shape to its net.

(a) (b) (c) (d) (e) (f)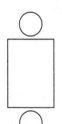

   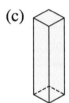 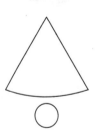

Finding the Volume of Other Shapes

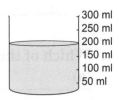

Here is another way to find the volume of shape.
Take a measuring glass and fill it with water up to the 200 mℓ mark.

Use fifty 1 centimetre cubes and fix them to make a cuboid with length 2 cm, breadth 5 cm, and height 5 cm.
What is the volume of the cuboid? _____ cu. cm.

Put the cuboid into the water in the measuring glass.
By how much has the level of water risen? _____ mℓ.

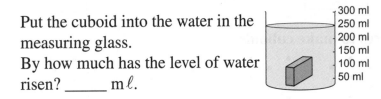

That means a cuboid of 50 cu. cm occupies the same space as 50 mℓ of water!

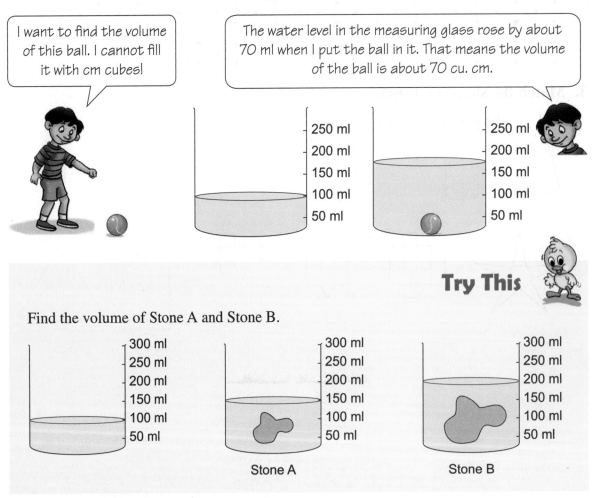

> I want to find the volume of this ball. I cannot fill it with cm cubes!

> The water level in the measuring glass rose by about 70 ml when I put the ball in it. That means the volume of the ball is about 70 cu. cm.

Try This

Find the volume of Stone A and Stone B.

Stone A

Stone B

Refer Maths Lab Activity on Page 186

Exercise 10.4

1. **By how many mℓ would the water level rise if you placed objects with these volumes in the measuring glass?**
   (a) 20 cu. cm   (b) 60 cu. cm   (c) 75 cu. cm

2. **What is the volume of objects that make the level of water rise by:**
   (a) 9 mℓ (b) 30 mℓ (c) 96 mℓ

3. **Use a measuring glass with 400 mℓ of water in it to find the volume of these objects.**

(a) Strawberry   (b) Onion   (c) Crayon

(d) Eraser   (e) 6 marbles   (f) One-rupee coin

(g) Dice   (h) Sharpener   (i) One marble

4. **Use the information that you got in 3 (e) and (f) to answer these questions.**
   (a) What is the volume of 12 marbles?
   (b) What is the volume of 160 one-rupee coins?

5. **If 9 five-rupee coins have a volume of 10 cu. cm, how many coins will be needed to make the water level rise by:**
   (a) 20 mℓ (b) 60 mℓ (c) 100 mℓ ?

CHAPTER CHECK-UP

1. Find the volume of these shapes.

(a) 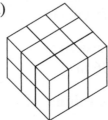   (b) 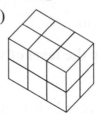   (c) 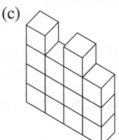   (d)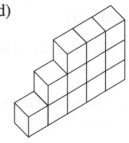

2. Use the shortcut to find the volume of these cuboids.

(a)   (b)    (c)    (d)

3. Which of these nets can be made into cubes?

(a)    (b) 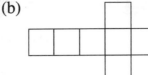   (c) 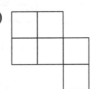   (d)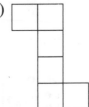

4. What is the volume of an object which makes the level of water in a measuring glass rise by 30 mℓ?

5. Complete the cuboids.

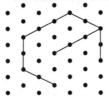   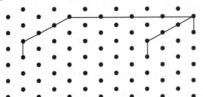

6. (a) A hole dug in the ground is 5 m long, 3 m broad, and 6 m deep. Find the volume of earth that was removed.

    (b) Find the volume of a cubic box whose sides are 8 cm long.

    (c) A rectangular solid has a volume of 120 cu. cm. Its length is 6 cm and its breadth is 2 cm. What is its height?

    (d) A book is 15 cm long, 20 cm wide, and 2 cm thick. How much space does the book occupy?

WORKSHEET

The floor map of a house tells you about the placement of doors, windows, etc., in a house, but does not tell you how high the house is or how the house actually looks. Only a three-dimensional drawing of a house can give you an idea of that. Match the floor plans to the three-dimensional pictures alongside. The placement of the doors and windows as well as the shape of the house will help you decide.

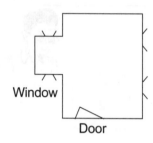

Window

Door

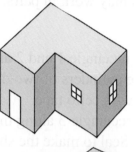

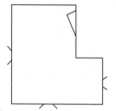

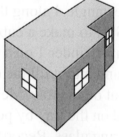

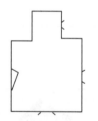

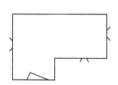

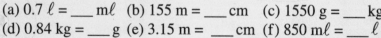

MATHS LAB ACTIVITY

Objective: To find the volume of containers of different shapes with the same area.

Materials Required: Measuring glass, bowl of sand, thick chart paper, cello tape, small tray

Preparation: Cut out 4 rectangular shapes of the same size from the chart paper (not smaller than 12 cm × 8 cm). Students may work in pairs.

> You can also use post cards or old cards.

Steps:

1. Take rectangle 1 and 2 and roll them to create cylinders of two different height. Seal with cello tape.
2. Fold rectangle 3 along the lines shown here. Seal to make the shape shown.
3. Fold rectangle 4 along the lines shown here. Seal to make a cuboid.
4. Hold up cylinder 1 on a small tray and pour sand into it till the top. Empty the sand out on the tray. Measure the amount of sand on the tray by pouring it into a measuring glass. Record the volume of the sand.
5. Repeat for all the shapes. Record all your findings.
6. What do you observe? Which is the shape with the greatest volume? Which is the shape with the least volume?

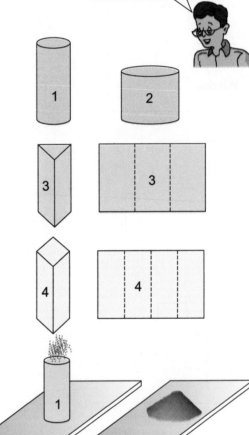

Record the Activity:

Shape	Volume
Shape 1	
Shape 2	
Shape 3	
Shape 4	

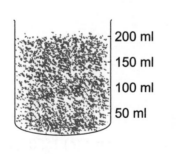

200 ml

150 ml

100 ml

50 ml

Time and Temperature

11

Looking Back

1. **Write how many minutes past the hour?**

_____   _____

2. **Fill in the blanks.**

   (a) 3:30 p.m. is written as _____ in the 24 hour clock.

   (b) 00:25 hours is written as _____ in the 12 hour clock.

   (c) 2 hours before midnight is 10:00 _____

   (d) 2 hours before 12 noon is 10:00 _____

   (e) There are _____ number of days between December 12 and January 11 (do not include January 11).

   (f) There are _____ number of days between March 23 and May 18 (include May 18).

3. (a) A play that started at 5:45 p.m. was 2 hours 30 minutes long. When did it get over?

   (b) Another play that started at 6:30 p.m. got over at 8:55 p.m. How long was the play?

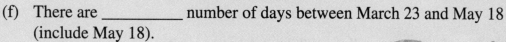

> ## Remember
>
> Time is always written with two dots between the hour and minutes.
>   8.30 ×
>   8:30 ✓

Time

Converting from One Unit to Another

Just like we had converted the units of measurement in Chapter 8, we can also convert different units of time.

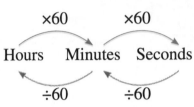

Multiply to change from a bigger unit to a smaller unit.

Hours   Minutes   Seconds

×60   ×60

÷60   ÷60

Divide to change from a smaller unit to a bigger unit.

Converting from a bigger unit to a smaller unit

(a) 4 hours = ___?___ minutes
4 × 60 = 240
4 hours = 240 minutes

(b) $2\frac{1}{2}$ minutes = ___?___ seconds
2 × 60 = 120 seconds
$\frac{1}{2}$ minute = 30 seconds
120 + 30 = 150 seconds
$2\frac{1}{2}$ minutes = 150 seconds

Try This

(a) 3 min = _____ seconds

(b) $2\frac{1}{2}$ hours = _____ minutes

Converting from a smaller unit to a bigger unit

(a) 920 minutes = ? hours

```
          1 5  → hours
    60)9 2 0
      − 6 0
        3 2 0
      − 3 0 0
          2 0  → minutes
```

920 minutes = 15 hours 20 minutes

Try This

(a) 720 sec = _____ min   (b) 400 min = _____ h _____ min

1. **Change to minutes.**
   (a) 8 hours
   (b) 11 hours
   (c) 7 hours
   (d) 9 h 20 min
   (e) 3 h 12 min
   (f) 4 h 42 min

2. **Change to hours and minutes.**
   (a) 720 min
   (b) 132 min
   (c) 130 min
   (d) 360 min
   (e) 410 min
   (f) 500 min

3. **Change to seconds.**
   (a) 13 min
   (b) 5 min
   (c) 26 min
   (d) $10\frac{1}{2}$ min
   (e) 15 min
   (f) 45 min

4. **Change to minutes and seconds.**
   (a) 840 sec
   (b) 480 sec
   (c) 280 sec
   (d) 600 sec
   (e) 93 sec
   (f) 950 sec

5. **Application in real life.**

   (a) A television programme had 11 minutes of advertisements in it. How many seconds were the advertisements for?

   (b) It takes Manisha 38 seconds to climb up the steps of her house. In one week if she spends 504 seconds doing this, how many minutes has she spent climbing up the steps?

   (c) An advertisement on radio lasted for 30 seconds. If the same advertisement is played daily for 10 days, for how many minutes will it be played?

   (d) A machine takes 3 seconds to fix the cap on a bottle of sauce. It has worked for 15 minutes. How many caps has it fixed? (**Hint:** *Convert the minutes to seconds first.*)

   (e) Smriti jogged for $1\frac{1}{2}$ hours on Monday and 90 minutes on Tuesday. On which day did she jog longer?

Project

Many world and olympic sports records are made with differences of even less than a second. For example, Usain Bolt of Jamaica won the 100 m race at the Beijing Olympics with 9.69 seconds. That is less than 10 seconds! Find other similar sports records and list them in your notebook.

Theme: It is a Holiday!

(a)  Ruchi and her family went for a weekend holiday to Mussorie. The train journey from Delhi to Dehradun was 5 hours 50 minutes. After that a taxi took 1 hour 45 minutes to Mussorie. How long did they spend travelling?

5 h 50 min + 1 h 45 min = ?
5 + 1 = _____ h
50 + 45 = _____ min
95 min is the same as _____ h _____ min
6 h + 1 h 35 min = _____ h _____ min
They spent _____ hours _____ minutes travelling.

95 min
60 min   35 min
(1 h)

(b) Raghav and his brother Apoorva played tennis for 2 h 10 min on Saturday and 1 h 40 minutes on Sunday. How much longer did they play on Saturday?
2 h 10 min – 1 h 40 min = ?
2 h 10 min is the same as 1 h 70 min
1 h 70 min – 1 h 40 min = _____ min
They played for _____ minutes longer on Saturday.

There are not enough minutes. So change 1 hour to minutes.

(c)  Ruchi is 10 years 5 months old and her brother is 7 years 9 months old. How much older is Ruchi?
10 years 5 months – 7 years 9 months = ?
10 years 5 months is the same as 9 years 17 months.
9 years 17 months – 7 years 9 months = ?
9 years – 7 years = _____ years
17 months – 9 months = _____ months
Ruchi is _____ years _____ months older than her brother.

Regroup 1 year to 12 months. So 5 + 12 = 17 months.

Exercise 11.2

1. (a) 5 min 30 sec + 5 min 30 sec   (b) 1 min 20 sec + 3 min 45 sec
    (c) 2 h 25 min + 45 min   (d) 1 h 40 m + 1 h 40 min
    (e) 3 years 7 months + 4 years 5 months   (f) 10 years 5 months + 11 years 7 months

2. (a) 8 min 10 sec – 7 min 2 sec   (b) 13 min – 5 min 35 sec
    (c) 9 h 20 min – 3 h 40 min   (d) 8 h 40 min – 3 h 50 min
    (e) 5 years 3 months – 2 years 3 months   (f) 8 years 6 months – 6 years 8 months

3. **Application in real life.**

   (a) Anisha practised for her school elocution competition for 35 minutes on one day and 45 minutes on the next day. How long did she practise in all?

   (b) Harish went to school for 11 years 6 months and college for 5 years 9 months. How many years of education is that?

   (c) A postman delivered parcels for 2 hours 15 minutes and letters for 3 hours 45 minutes. For how long was he on the beat?

   (d) Jayashree could swim a particular length in 3 minutes 22 seconds. After some practice, she could swim the same length in 2 minutes 40 seconds. By how much time had her speed improved?

   (e) A normal train from Chennai to Bangalore takes 6 hours 10 minutes. The Shatabdi Express takes 4 hours 45 minute. How much time do you save by travelling on the Shatabdi?

Project

If today is Wednesday, what will be the day 17 days from today?

Sun	0
Mon	1
Tue	2
Wed	3
Thu	4
Fri	5
Sat	6

- Wednesday is 3 on the table.
- 17 + 3 = 20.
- 20 ÷ 7 (number of days in a week) = 2, remainder = 6.
- 6 is Saturday on the table.
- 17 days from today, Wednesday will be Saturday.

Now try it out yourself with other dates.

Finding the Starting Time or Finishing Time

To Find the Finishing Time

Ajay started the marathon race at 8:30 a.m. He finished 3 hours 32 minutes later. What time did he finish?

Starting time—8:30 a.m.
Finishing time—after 3 hours 32 minutes.
To find out what time Ajay finished the marathon, we need to **add the elapsed time to the starting time**.

Starting time + Elapsed time = Finishing time

The time spent during an event or activity is the duration of the event or 'elapsed time'. We have to **count forward** to find the finishing time.

8:30 + 3 hours 32 minutes = ?

Count in parts ⟶ 8:30 a.m. + 3 hours = 11:30 a.m.

11:30 a.m. + 32 minutes = 12:02 p.m.

Answer: Ajay finished the marathon at 12:02 p.m.

Common Mistake!

11:45 a.m. + 30 minutes
= 12:15 a.m. ✗
= 12:15 p.m. ✓

To Find the Starting Time

Devesh woke up at 7:30 a.m. after sleeping for 8 hours 45 minutes. What time did he go to bed?

Here, we have the finishing time and the elapsed time, but not the starting time.

Finishing time – Elapsed time = Starting time

We have to **count backwards** from the finishing time to find the starting time.

7:30 a.m. – 8 hours 45 minutes = ?

Count back in parts.

7:30 a.m. – 7 hours = 12:30 a.m.
12:30 a.m. – 1 hour = 11:30 p.m.
11:30 p.m. – 45 minutes = 10:45 p.m.
Answer: Devesh had gone to bed at 10:45 p.m.

Common Mistake!

12:30 p.m. – 45 min
= 11:45 p.m. ✗
= 11:45 a.m. ✓

Common Mistake!

12 p.m. ✗
12 noon ✓

Calculating Days

Sometimes we may need to find out for how many days a certain event or activity took place.

Common Mistake!

12 a.m. ✗
12 midnight ✓

To Find the Finishing Date

Sudha started reading a book on 7th August. She finished reading it 32 days later. On which date did she finish?

Starting date—7th August
Duration—32 days
Finishing date—?

Starting date + Duration = Finishing date

We need to **count forward** to find the finishing date. We can count in parts.
7th August to 31st August = 25 days (31 – 7 = 24 + 1 = 25)
1st September to 7th September = 7 days (25 + 7 = 32 days)
Answer: Sudha finished reading the book on 7th September.

To Find the Starting Date

Lakshmi returned from her 45-day holiday on 10th July.
When did her holiday begin?

Return date—10th July
Duration of holiday—45 days
Starting date—?

Count back 45 days from 10th July.
10th July to 1st July   = 10 days
30th June to 1st June   = 30 days
31st May to 27th May =   5 days
                          _____
                          45 days

Answer: Lakshmi started her holiday on 27th May.

Challenge

Divya has three clocks in her house. The problem is that not one of them keeps
the right time! One clock is 15 minutes fast, another is half an hour fast, and
the third one is 10 minutes slow. The clocks in Divya's house are shown below,
but they are not in any particular order. Can you figure out what is the right time now?

10:50   10:35    10:10

Exercise 11.3

1. **Fill in the missing information. Use a.m. or p.m.**

	Starting time	Elapsed time	Finishing time
(a)	1:05 p.m.	4 hours 40 minutes	
(b)	11:15 a.m.	2 hours 45 minutes	
(c)	9:30 a.m.	5 hours 45 minutes	
(d)		5 hours 15 minutes	6:00 p.m.
(e)		3 hours 20 minutes	3:20 a.m.
(f)		7 hours 25 minutes	10:10 p.m.

2.

	Starting date	Duration	Finishing date
(a)	21st December	26 days	
(b)	19th November	25 days	
(c)	3rd March	47 days	
(d)		13 days	2nd April
(e)		28 days	10th January
(f)		40 days	24th June

3. **Application in real life.**

(a) Apoorva's school Sports day is on March 20th. He wants to start practising 30 days earlier. When should he start? (Take February to have 28 days.)

(b) Nikhil's birthday party started at 11:45 a.m. and finished 3 hours 40 minutes later. When did his friends leave?

(c)  Meera started knitting a muffler on Independence Day. If she completed it in 25 days, on what day did she finish it?

(d) Madhur joined a 2-week driving class that got over on September 3rd. When did it begin?

(e) Prachi started practising the *veena* at 1:15 p.m. and finished 1 hour 20 minutes later. What time did she finish?

Measurement of Temperature

Temperature is the measure of how hot or how cold something is. We use thermometers to measure temperature.

Celsius Scale

The metric system uses a scale called the **Celsius scale** in the thermometer. On the Celsius scale, **water freezes at 0°C and boils at 100°C.**

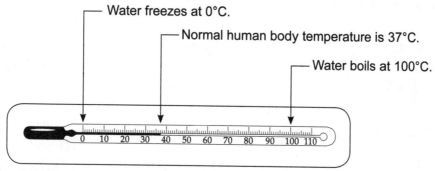

— Water freezes at 0°C.

— Normal human body temperature is 37°C.

— Water boils at 100°C.

Knowledge of outdoor temperature helps us in judging the weather conditions.

0°C – 10°C: Cold weather   20°C – 25°C: Mild weather   30°C – 35°C: Hot weather
10°C – 20°C: Cool weather   25°C – 30°C: Warm weather   35°C – 40°C and above:
                                                                                                    Very hot weather

Project

Find out the highest summer temperature and the lowest winter temperature in your city. Use the information above to decide what kind of weather your city experiences. Find out today's temperature. What is the weather today?

We use a '**clinical**' thermometer which shows a range from **35°C to 42°C** to measure body temperature. The longer marks between two numbers show the halfway point or 0.5°C.

The temperature on the thermometer is brought down to below 35°C before checking a person's fever.

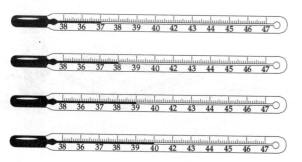

Normal body temperature 37°C

Low fever _____°C

High fever _____°C

Very high fever _____°C

Exercise 11.4

1. Circle the temperature that is close to the situation described.

(a) Warm day
(35°C)/5°C

(b) Hot bath
42°C/10°C

(c) Hot milk
45°C/15°C

(d) Cold drink
5°C/30°C

(e) Ice
0°C/100°C

(f) Feverish person
38.5°C/35.8°C

2. Read these temperatures.

(a)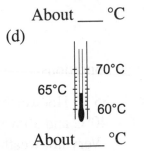

About ___ °C

(b)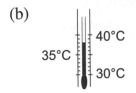

About ___ °C

(c)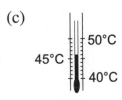

About ___ °C

(d)

70°C
65°C
60°C

About ___ °C

(e)

20°C
15°C
10°C

About ___ °C

(f)

80°C
75°C
70°C

About ___ °C

3. Application in real life.

(a) Shristi places a pan filled with ice on the gas stove. If the temperature increases by 5°C every minute, how long will it take for the water to boil?

(b) Shristi's father is boiling water on the gas stove. The water is 18°C less than the boiling point. How hot is the water?

Project

Use the newspaper to find the temperatures of 6 cities in India. Find out:
(a) Which is the coolest city?
(b) Which is the hottest city?
(c) What is the difference between the two temperatures?

CHAPTER CHECK-UP

1. **Fill in the blanks.**
   (a) 3 h 20 min = _____ min
   (b) 560 min = _____ h _____ min
   (c) $11\frac{1}{2}$ min = _____ sec
   (d) 980 sec = _____ min _____ sec
   (e) 15 min – 3 min 20 sec = _____
   (f) 4 years 7 months – 2 years 8 months = _____
   (g) 2 h 40 min + 3 h 30 min = _____

2. **Find the time.**
   (a) 3 h 20 min after 11 : 45 a.m.
   (b) 4 h 50 min before 7 : 20 p.m.

3. **Find the date.**
   (a) 13 days after 28th August
   (b) 25 days before 16th November

4. **Read the temperature.**

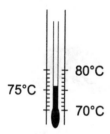

5. (a) On Monday Amar took 1 hour 40 minutes to complete his homework. On Tuesday he took 50 minutes more to complete his homework. How long did he take to complete his homework on Tuesday?

   (b) On Monday Anu practicsed singing for 2 hours 10 minutes. On Tuesday she practised for 1 hour 40 minutes. How much longer did she practise on Monday than Tuesday?

WORKSHEET

You may have often heard of fish, snakes, and frogs being referred to as **cold-blooded** animals. They are called cold-blooded because their body temperature changes according to their surroundings.

A salmon can have a body temperature ranging from 0°C to 20°C.

A frog's body temperature ranges from 7°C to 30°C.

A lizard's body temperature ranges from 18°C to 45°C.

This worksheet integrates Mathematics and Science.

Human beings, birds, and many other animals are said to be **warm-blooded**. The temperature of their bodies does not change with a change in outside temperature. These are the normal body temperatures of warm-blooded creatures:

Bat   – 28°C
Hedgehog   – 35°C
Human being   – 37°C
Spiny ant eater – 30°C
Bird   – 40°C

Answer these questions:

1. How much warmer is bird's body than a bat's body?
2. How much colder is the body temperature of a spiny anteater as compared to a hedgehog?
3. By how many degrees can the body temperature of a lizard increase or decrease?
4. What is the minimum body temperature of a salmon?
5. What is the maximum body temperature of a frog?

Keeping in Touch

What is the area and perimeter of these shapes?

(a)

7 m

12 m

(b) 9 m

9 m   9 m

9 m

Mapping Skills

Nandu was writing to his pen friend Jeanne, who lives in Paris, France, to explain to her where he lived. This is how he did it.

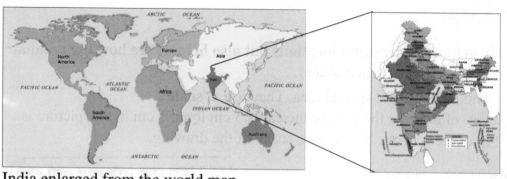

India enlarged from the world map.

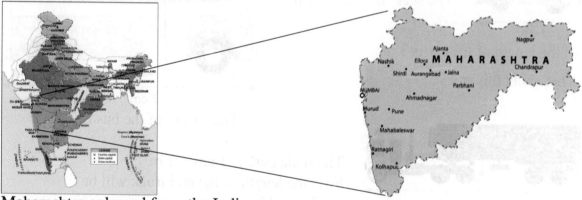

Maharashtra enlarged from the India map.

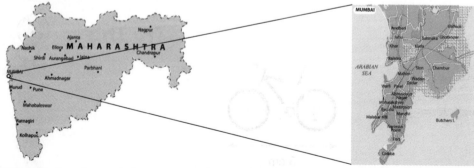

Mumbai enlarged from the Maharashtra map.

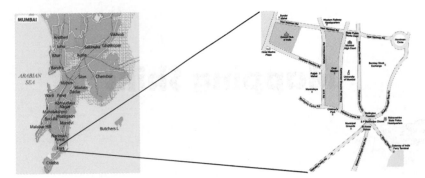

South Mumbai enlarged from Mumbai map.

From this Jeanne understood that Nandu lived in a country called _____, in the state of _____, in the city of _____, and in the _____ locality.

Scales in Maps

Maps not only help us understand locations but also help us see how big or small places are in comparison to other places.

Maps do this with the help of a special idea. They use a 'scale'.
This is the picture of a car. In the picture the car is 3 cm long. 1 cm in the picture is the same as 1 m of the real car. This is the 'scale' of the drawing.

The scale is 1 cm = 1 m

3 cm

So the length of the car is 3 m.

What about this truck?

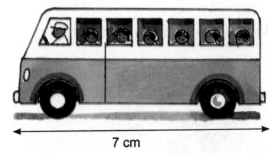

The length of the bus is 7 m.

6 cm

The scale here is 1 cm = 2 m
So is the length of the real truck will be
6×2 m = 12 m.

Try This

Scale is 1 cm = $\frac{1}{2}$ m

Length of the bicycle = ____

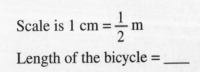

3 cm

Project

Use an atlas. Find out the different scales used on the maps. Make a note of the scales used on the maps of the world, India, and the state you live in. Can you find a map of your city in the atlas? Make a note of that too. If the map of the world and the map of India are about the same size in the atlas, what do you notice about the two scales used? Why did it need to be like that?

This is a photograph of Nandu. He wants to send it to Jeanne, but since it is too small he takes it to a photography shop to get it blown up to double its size.

4 cm

2 cm

8 cm

4 cm

The larger picture has twice the length and width of the original picture. Measure the diagonals of the two pictures. What do you notice? .

What is the area of the first picture?

Is the area of the second picture double that of the first picture? Calculate the areas before you answer. What is the relationship? Why has it happened?

Diagonals

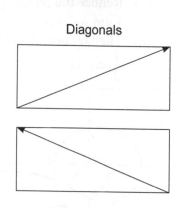

Nandu also reduced the size of the original photo by half so that he could use it for the school identity card.

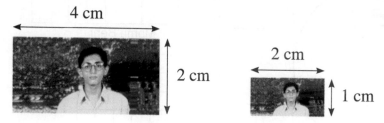

4 cm

2 cm

2 cm

1 cm

Find the area of the new picture. Is it half that of the original picture? What about the diagonal?

A

B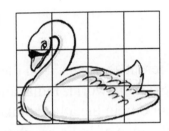

C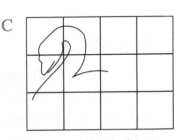

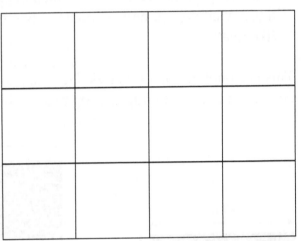

Nandu's younger brother has drawn this picture of a swan. Nandu can either increase or reduce the size of the drawing by taking the help of squares. Here he has copied the picture in the same size; so the scale that is 1 cm square in the original picture (A) is 1 cm square in the copy (B). Complete the picture by copying it square to square in C.

Use the squares on the right to enlarge the same picture using the scale 1 cm = 2 cm.

Try This

(a) Reduce the picture of Papa Bear to Mama Bear by copying the picture on the 1 cm squares.

(b) Then reduce the picture of Mama Bear to that of Baby Bear by copying it on to the $\frac{1}{2}$ cm squares.

Papa Bear

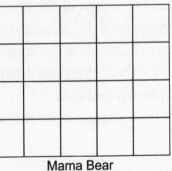

Mama Bear

Baby Bear

Project

Take any cartoon picture from a book and draw cm squares over the original picture. Then draw 2 cm squares on a blank sheet of paper. Copy the picture into this to make it double the size.

Try the same idea to make the picture 3 times larger.

Keys in Maps

This is a map of Nandu's classroom. The 'key' tells us the meaning of the different symbols used in the map.

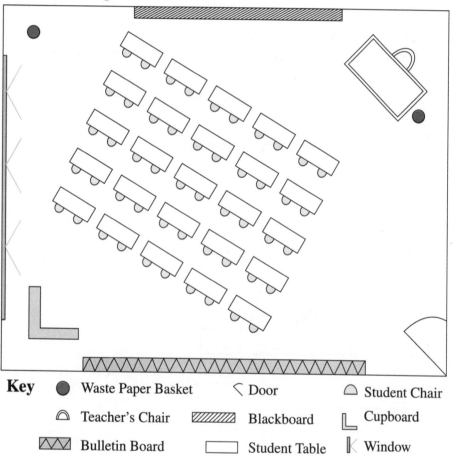

Key ● Waste Paper Basket   〈 Door   ⌂ Student Chair

⌂ Teacher's Chair   ▨ Blackboard   L Cupboard

▨ Bulletin Board   ☐ Student Table   ⊩ Window

Study the map with the help of the key and then answer these questions.

1. Why do you think the teacher's desk has been placed in the corner?
2. Is the seating arrangement for the students a good one? Say yes or no with reasons.

Did you know that while writing the light source should be on your left if you are right handed?

3. Nandu sits in the second last row, middle seat. Use a pencil on the map to draw the shortest route he can take to go to the teacher's table.
4. Can you think of another arrangement so that all the students can move around easily in the classroom? Draw it in your notebook.
5. Can you think of an arrangement more suited to group work? Draw it in your notebook.
6. Which object in the classroom is in the corner diagonally opposite to the teacher's table?
7. If you take a left turn as soon as you enter the classroom which object will you be approaching?
8. Which waste paper basket will the child, who sits in the last row, extreme right, use? Why?

This is a map of Nandu's school.
Study the map, the key, and the scale carefully before answering the questions.

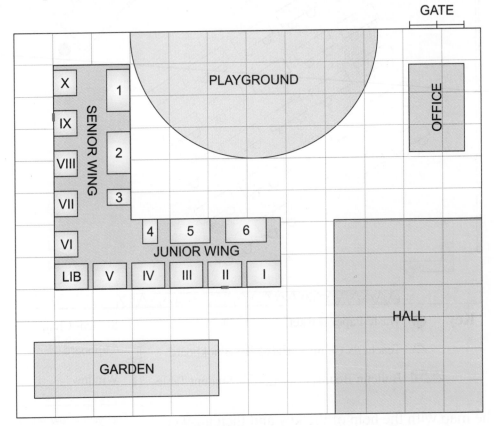

Key   LIB   Library   3, 4   Toilets   I to X   classrooms
         1   Staff Room   5   Music Room
         2   Science Lab   6   Maths Lab

1. Has the school office been placed well in the school plan? Why?
2. When you enter the school from the junior wing side, why are the classrooms on the left of the school building and the activity rooms on the right?

3. If you stand in the garden facing the Junior wing, what do you have to your right?
4. A red line has been marked to show the windows in Classes II and IX. Draw a red line to show the window in all the classrooms.
5. Use the map of Nandu's classroom on Page 203 to help you mark answers a, b, c on the map on this page.
   (a) A blue line to show the blackboard in Class IV.
   (b) A green dot to mark the teacher's table in Class X.
   (c) A yellow line to mark the door in Class VII.

Direction in Maps

Another important thing that maps show you is **direction**.
You must have often seen this on many maps.
You know that they stand for North, East, South, and West.
Red, Blue, Yellow, Black, and Green are marked on this grid.

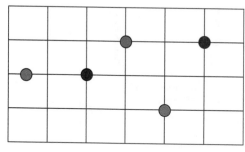

Black is to the east of Red
Orange is to the west of Blue
Green is the southernmost colour.

I remember my directions starting from the North and going clockwise with this sentence—
Nine Elephants Shift Wood.

Try This

Answer the questions given below by studying the map of the Punjab.

1. Which is the northern most town?
2. Name the town to the south of Faridkot.
3. Rupnagar is to the _____ of Ludhiana.
4. Which town is to the most extreme west of Punjab?
5. Which town is to the immediate east of Sangrur?
6. If you were travelling from Moga to Amritsar, in which direction would you be travelling?

This is the area Nandu lives in Mumbai.

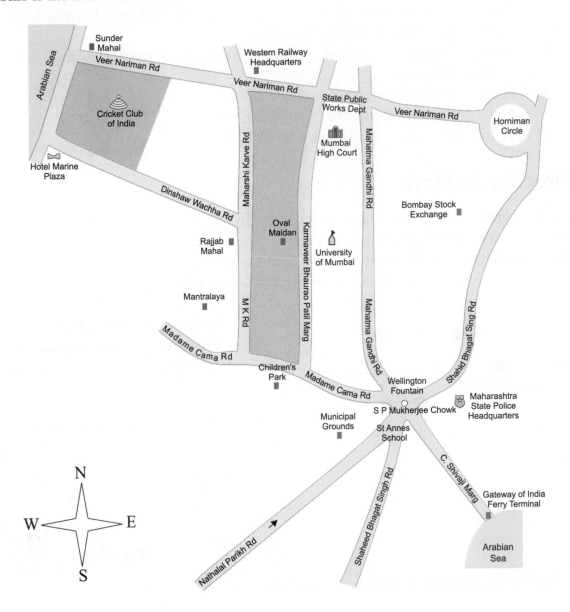

1. Mark these on the map.
   (a) Cricket Club of India
   (c) University of Mumbai
   (e) Gateway of India
   (b) Mumbai High Court
   (d) Oval maidan
   (f) Horniman Circle
2. Name the roads that form the shortest route from Horniman Circle to Gateway of India. Which direction will you move in if you take those roads?
3. If you are walking on Karmaveer Bhaurao Patil Marg in the northward direction, you will have the _____ to your left and the _____ and _____ to your right.
4. Name the roads radiating from SP Mukherjee chowk. Which two pairs of roads form the smallest angle with the Chowk as the common point?

5. If you are walking on Veer Nariman Road towards the sea, in which direction will you be walking?

6. A small portion of the map has been further reduced to 1 cm squares. Can you identify the place on the larger map? Enlarge this to double its size by copying it on to 2 cm squares.

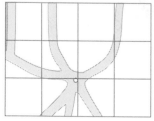

Use the map of India to answer these questions.

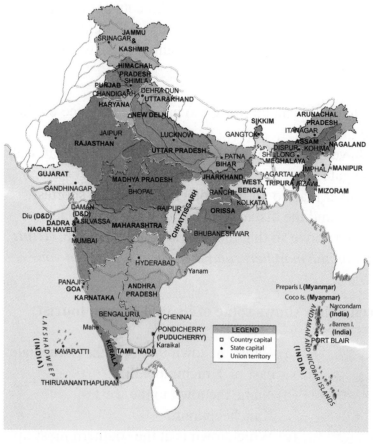

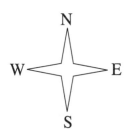

Scale 1 cm = 320 km

1. Name the state at the southernmost part of India.
2. Name the state at the eastern most part of India.
3. Name all the states on the west coast of India.
4. Which state is to the west of Orissa?
5. Which state is to the east of Karnataka?
6. Keep the scale in mind and use estimation to answer these questions.

   (a) The approximate distance between Goa and Delhi.
   (b) The approximate distance between Puducherry and Daman.
   (c) Which state is approximately twice the size of Sikkim?
   (d) Name four small states that are neighbours and have approximately the same area.
   (e) Orissa is approximately half/double the size of Andhra Pradesh (cross out the incorrect one).

Use a centimetre scale to help you in Question 6. You can also use a string with knots at every 1 cm.

CHAPTER CHECK-UP

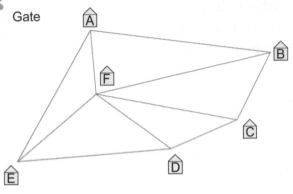

Gate

This is a map of the Khanna brothers' farm. Each brother has his own cottage in different parts of the farm. Raju, the postman, comes to deliver mail to them every day. He enters and exits the farm at the gate near A's cottage. Using a scale of 1 cm = 100 m, use a ruler to measure and answer these questions.

1. (a) What is the shortest route that Raju can take to C? What is the distance on the map and what is the actual distance?

    (b) On one day only B and D have mail. What the least distance that Raju can walk to them and back out of the gate?

    (c) The day that Raju has to deliver mail to all the brothers he uses the shortest route possible. Find that route and the distance he has to walk to do that.

    (d) Make a copy of the map given above so that the map is double the size. (***Hint:*** *you can draw 1 cm squares on the map here, and then 2 cm squares in your notebook to copy into.*)

2. **The map of Tamil Nadu given below shows some of its well-known tourist destinations.**

    (a) Name the town that is to the immediate east of Tiruchirappalli.

    (b) Name the town to the west of Kancheepuram.

    (c) Which town is at the southern most tip?

    (d) If you are travelling from Puducherry to Chennai in which direction will you be going?

WORKSHEET

The map below shows the route that Mahatma Gandhi took on his famous Dandi march to defy the British salt tax. The march began on March 12th 1930 from his ashram at Sabarmati in Gujarat and ended on 6th April at Dandi.

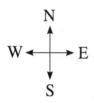

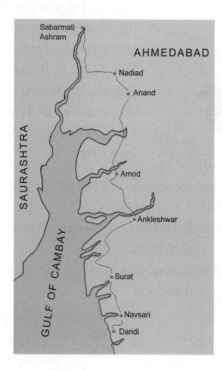

1. How many days was the march?
2. In which direction did Gandhiji walk on the salt march?
3. Some of his followers came from Goa. In which direction did they travel to meet Gandhiji at Sabarmati? (Use the India map on Page 207.)
4. Madhya Pradesh is to the _____ of Gujarat and Rajasthan is to its _____ (Use the map of India on Page 207.)
5. Which states does someone who is travelling from Kolkata to Sabarmati have to cross to get there? (Use the map of India on Page 207.)

Keeping in Touch
Find the volume of this box.

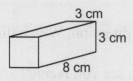

3 cm
3 cm
8 cm

LOOKING BEYOND

Enrichment Time

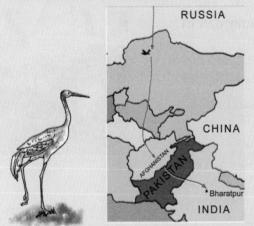

RUSSIA

CHINA

AFGHANISTAN

PAKISTAN

Bharatpur

INDIA

Birds from cold climates fly long distances in the same direction year after year to nest in a warm place. For several years the now-endangered Siberian cranes came from Russia to nest in the Bharatpur Bird Sanctuary in Rajasthan. The map shows that the birds first flew south towards Afghanistan and then turned towards the east to Bharatpur. We call this the **south-east** direction.

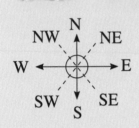

If the direction is between the north and east, it is called North-East direction.

If the direction is between the south and west it is the _____ direction.

If the direction is between the north and west it is the _____ direction.

Try this

In which direction is the minute hand pointing?

Monkeys

Elephants

Bears

Lions

The elephant enclosure is in the _____ corner of the zoo.

The north west corner of the zoo has the _____ cages.

Activity Bag

Draw a large square on the floor with chalk as shown. Four students may stand on the square with a card in hand showing each of the 4 directions. One student may stand in the centre. Slips may be prepared or the teacher may call out instructions for the student in the centre. For example,

(a) Stand facing north. Take a quarter turn in the clockwise direction. Which direction are you facing?

(b) Face West. Take two half turns in the clockwise direction. Which direction are you facing?

(c) Face South. Take a quarter turn. Which direction are you facing?

Handling Data

Looking Back

1. **The bar graph below shows the number of books read by students during the summer vacations.**

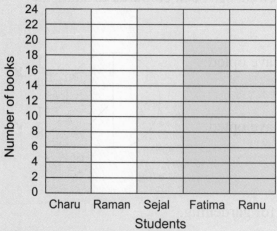

Vertical axis: Number of books (0, 2, 4, 6, 8, 10, 12, 14, 16, 18, 20, 22, 24)

Horizontal axis — Students: Charu, Raman, Sejal, Fatima, Ranu

(a) What does the vertical scale show? _____

(b) Which student read the most number of books? _____

(c) Which two students read the same number of books? _____

(d) How many more books did Charu read than Sejal? _____

2.

This circle graph shows where Shariq spent his summer holidays. Read the graph to answer the questions.

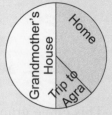

Circle graph labels: Grandmother's House, Home, Trip to Agra

(a) Where did Shariq spend the maximum number of days of his vacation? _____

(b) Where did he spend the least number of days? _____

(c) Was he at home more or less than at his grandmother's house? _____

More about Circle Graphs

Circle graphs show all the parts of a whole. Here the whole consists of all the 24 students of class V-B.

The table shows the hobby classes that the students chose for the term. The circle graph shows the same information.

Music	12 students
Art	6 students
Gardening	3 students
Sewing	3 students

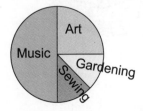

What is the total number of students shown in the graph? _____

 12 out of 24 students have opted for music. That is half the students have opted for music. So $\frac{1}{2}$ the circle has been coloured to show the information.

 6 out of 24 is $\frac{6}{24}$ or $\frac{1}{4}$ students have opted for art.

 3 out of 24 is $\frac{3}{24}$ or $\frac{1}{8}$ students have opted for sewing.

Common Mistake!

 3 out of 24 or $\frac{1}{8}$ students opted for gardening.

$\frac{1}{4}$ ✗

$\frac{1}{8}$ ✓

Try This

 In a class of 36 students. 9 students learn singing. Represent this by colouring the graph.

 **Exercise 13.1**

1. This circle graph shows how Rishabh spent his day. A day has 24 hours. The circle has been divided into 8 equal parts with dotted lines. So each part represents 3 hours. You can fill in the details on the table with the help of the circle graph.

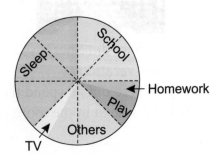

6 hours	
9 hours	
1 hour	Homework
2 hours	
5 hours	
1 hour	

2. 100 people were asked which kind of movies were their favourite. Look at the table that gives their replies, and colour and label the circle graph accordingly.

Adventure	24
Comedy	20
Mystery	20
Drama	36

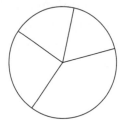

3. This circle graph shows the votes for the class election. If there are 40 students in the class, estimate the number of votes each person who stood for the election got.

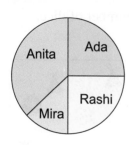

(a) (i) Ada   (*Hint:* $\frac{1}{4}$ *of 40*)

    (ii) Rashi

    (iii) Mira   (*Hint:* $\frac{1}{8}$ *of 40*)

    (iv) Anita

(b) Who won the election?

(c) Which two students got the same number of votes? How many more votes did Rashi get than Mira?

Tally Marks

Bhupen was trying to find out from his classmates the most popular choice for a class trip. He used 'tally marks' to record their answer.

| is 1 || is 2 |||| is 4

卌 is 5   卌 || is 7   卌 卌 is 10

Choices	Tally marks	Number of students
Garden	卌 III	8
Beach	卌 卌 卌	
Zoo	卌 卌 II	
Planetarium	卌 IIII	
Museum	卌 II	

1. Fill in the last column in the above table.
2. How many students are there in the class?
3. Which is the most popular place for the picnic?
4. Which is the least popular place for the picnic?
5. How many more students prefer the zoo to the planetarium?

Try This

Use the pictures below to build a table using tally marks to find the number of dice, candles, caps, and balls.

Project

Copy this table in your notebook. Collect the information with the help of tally marks.

Students in Class V who have brothers and sisters.

	Tally marks	Number of students
No brothers or sisters		
Only brothers		
Only sisters		
Both brothers and sisters		

1. **Complete the tally chart.**

    Number of hours the students of Class V watch TV in a day.

Number of hours	Tally marks	Number of students
Less than $\frac{1}{2}$ hour	II	
Between $\frac{1}{2}$ and 1 hour	IIII IIII IIII	
Between 1 and 2 hours	IIII IIII IIII II	
Between 2 and 3 hours	IIII IIII	
More than 3 hours	III	

2. **Build a tally chart using these pictures.**

    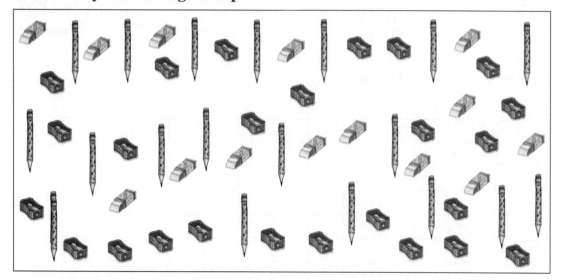

3. **Use the pictograph given below to build a bar graph and a tally chart in your notebook.**

Number of shapes				
■	■ ■ ■ ■			
●	● ● ● ● ●			
▲	▲ ▲ ▲ ▲ ▲ ▲ ▲			
	Each symbol stands for 2 shapes			

Challenge

Shefali has made these marks monthwise to count the number of days to her birthday. On which date did she start the tally marks? On which date is her birthday?

| ||| |||| | |||| |||| |||| |||| |||| ||| | |||| |||| || |

(Hint: First count the numbers in the middle to find which month it is.)

Line Graphs

Mrs Menon kept a record of her baby's height from the time he was born till he was 12 months of age. She put a dot on the chart every time she took his height.

0 month (at birth)	–	50 cm
1 month	–	55 cm
3 months	–	65 cm
6 months	–	70 cm
9 months	–	75 cm
12 months	–	80 cm

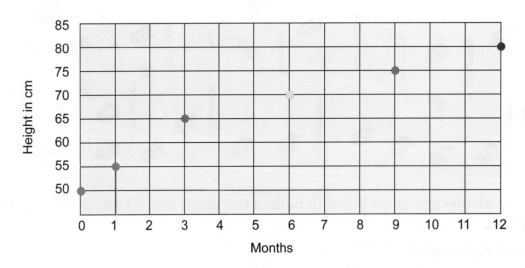

Can you see how the dots have been put?

The first vertical line shows 0 months. The first horizontal line shows 50 cm. The red vertical line shows 1 month and the red horizontal line shows 55 cm. The dot has been put on the crossing of the two lines. Check how the other dots have been put before you go further. Use a ruler to help you.

Join the dots to make a line graph. Use the graph to answer the questions.

(a) What was the baby's height at birth? _____

(b) How many cm did he grow in his first month? _____

(c) How many cm did he grow from his birth to his third month? _____

(d) How many cm did he grow from 3 months to 6 months? _____

(e) What was his height at 12 months? _____

This graph of the baby's weight shows you the baby's weight in kg for the first 12 months after birth. Answer the questions by looking only at the graph.

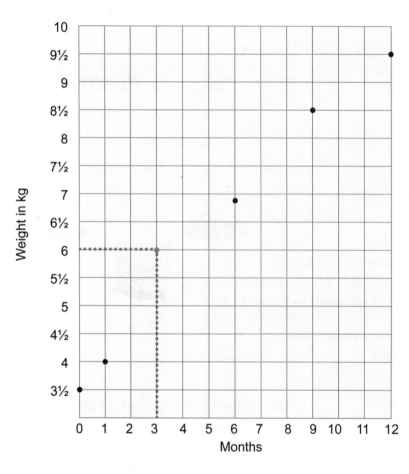

Use a ruler to help you read the graph. For example, the vertical green line shows the baby's age as 3 months and the horizontal green line shows that he was 6 kg then.

1. How much do you think the baby weighed when he was born? _____

2. What was his weight at 1 month? _____

3. Can you estimate his weight at 6 months? _____

4. What was his weight at 12 months? _____

5. How many kg did he gain in his first 3 months? _____

CHAPTER CHECK-UP

1. **The circle graph shows the number of hours Anshuman spends studying different subjects every week out of total study time of 12 hours.**

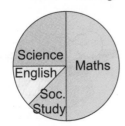

   (a) Give the fraction shown by the circle graph for each subject.
   (b) How many hours does he spend studying Maths every week?
   (c) How much time is spent on Science?
   (d) If he spends 3 hours studying English and Social Studies together, how much time does he spend on each?

2. **Favourite recess snack of students in Class V-A.**

Snack	Tally marks	Number
Sandwich	ЦН ЦН ЦН	
Chips	ЦН ЦН ЦН ЦН ЦН I	
Samosa	ЦН ЦН ЦН	
Cake	ЦН II	

   (a) Which is the most popular snack in class?
   (b) Which is the least popular?
   (c) Which two snacks are equally popular?
   (d) How many more children like chips than cake?
   (e) How many children are there in all in Class V-A?

3. **Study the graph and answer the questions.**

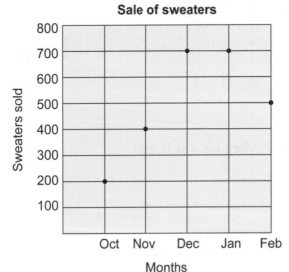

   (a) Which two months had the maximum sale of sweaters?
   (b) Which month had the least sale?
   (c) How many sweaters were sold in November?
   (d) How many less sweaters were sold in February than January?

218

WORKSHEET

The following data shows the number of years the first five presidents of India served their term. Complete the table and graph given below and answer the questions that follow.

President	From–to	Number of years
Dr Rajendra Prasad (RP)	1950–1962	12
Dr S. Radhakrishnan (SR)	1962–1967	5
Dr Zakir Husain (ZH)	1967–1969	
Shri V.V. Giri (VVG)	1969–1974	
Dr Fakhruddin Ali Ahmed (FAA)	1974–1977	

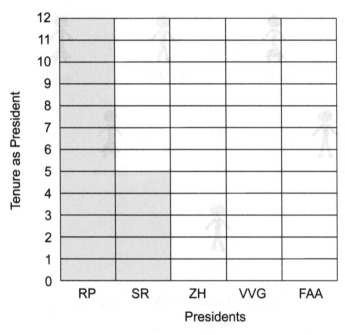

This worksheet integrates Mathematics and Social Studies.

Answer the following questions.

1. Who was the longest-serving president?
2. Who had the shortest term?
3. Which two presidents served for the same number of years? For how many years did each serve as president?
4. How many years did the first five presidents of India serve in all?

Keeping in Touch
(a) Find the time 2 hours 45 minutes after 11 : 15 p.m.
(b) Find the date 16 days before 3rd May.

LOOKING BEYOND

Enrichment Time

Kunal wanted to make his family tree. He used this outline.

Read Kunal's family tree with the help of this outline and answer the questions given below.

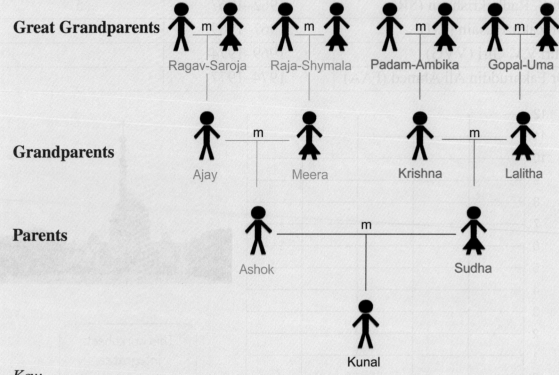

Key:

Red – Kunal's mother's side of the family

Blue – Kunal's father's side of the family

m – married

(a) How many grandparents does Kunal have?

(b) How many great grandparents?

(c) If Kunal is called the first generation in his family tree, and his great grandparents are 4th generation, what will the generation above theirs be called?

(d) From the pattern can you tell how many people in that generation?

(e) Name Kunal's mother's parents.

(f) Name Kunal's father's grandparents.

Activity Bag

Use the idea shown above to make your own family tree. Get photographs wherever possible and stick it on the family tree.

TEST YOUR SKILLS*

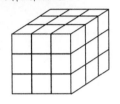

1. **Find the volume of these shapes.**

8 cm
10 cm
15 cm

2. **Fill in the empty boxes.**

    (a) **Starting time**   **Elapsed time**   **Finishing time**
        9:10 a.m.   3 h 35 min   _____
        _____   5 h 15 min   12:10 p.m.

    (b) **Starting date**   **Duration**   **Finishing date**
        27ᵗʰ November   35 days   _____
        _____   18 days   January 10ᵗʰ

3. **Match the following.**

    Warm day   6°C
    Cold milk   50°C
    Hot tea   35°C

4. **Use the map of India on Page 207 to find out:**

    (a) Which is the western most state of India?

    (b) Which states are to the south of Madhya Pradesh?

5. **Make a tally chart of the favourite writers of your classmates.**

6. **Study the graph to answer the following questions.**

Graph showing Shubha's test marks over 5 tests.

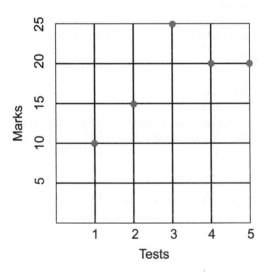

(a) Fill in the table

Test	Marks
1	
2	
3	
4	
5	

(b) Which test did Shubha do best in?

(c) What were her lowest marks?

(d) Which two tests did she get the same marks? How much was that?

* This is for Chapters 10, 11, 12, and 13.

221

ANSWERS TO SELECT QUESTIONS

Chapter 1 – Place Value

Exercise 1.1

1. Across:
   1. 10   6. 23,48,901   4. 99
   7. 976553200   8. 83,11,497

   Down:
   1. 19,99,998   2. 6,345,121   3. 38,63,659
   4. 9,00,000   5. 91,20,412

4. (a) 8,39,023   (b) 20,00,905   (c) 35,857
   (d) 83,00,900   (e) 4,37,19,000
6. (a) >   (b) >   (c) <   (d) <
7. (a) 11,12,589
   (b) 10,00,479
8. (a) Smallest – 1,12,36,789 Greatest – 9,98,76,321
   (b) Smallest – 1,00,03,457 Greatest – 7,77,54,310

Exercise 1.3

1. (a) 1350   (b) 2390   (c) 10,150
   (d) 92,410   (e) 7,83,090   (f) 11,000
2. (a) 18,600   (b) 75,300   (c) 87,000
   (d) 14,900   (e) 4,05,000
3. (a) 2,36,000   (b) 4,00,000   (c) 4,10,000
   (d) 36,000   (e) 9,78,000

Chapter Check-up

3. (a) 8,000   (b) 60,000   (c) 6,00,00,000
5. (a) 79,99,000   (b) 15,10,000
6. (a) 5,09,999   (b) 13,80,969

Worksheet

(1) Hindi (2) Sanskrit (3) Bengali (4) 5,00,00,000
(5) 50,000 (6) Hindi, Bengali, Telugu, Marathi, Tamil, and Urdu

Chapter 2 – The Four Operations

Exercise 2.1

1. (a) 31,629   (b) 1,41,717   (c) 1,14,781
   (d) 1,41,779   (e) 1,12,967   (f) 2,88,833
   (g) 2,91,544   (h) 2,14,097   (i) 1,86,500
2. (a)
   ```
     23456
   + 58557
   -------
     82013
   ```
   (b)
   ```
     72642
   + 75859
   -------
    148501
   ```
3. (a) 5781   (b) 14,897   (c) 8,60,500
   (d) 2,93,248.   (e) 11,397   (f) 13,220
   (g) 10,155   (h) 4804   (i) 59,113
2. (a)
   ```
     24635
   - 19431
   -------
      5204
   ```
   (b)
   ```
     77726
   - 15446
   -------
     62280
   ```

Exercise 2.2

1. (b) Profit; Rs 540   (c) Profit; Rs 540   (d) Loss; Rs 180

(e) Loss; Rs 75   (f) Profit; Rs 675   (g) Loss; Rs 95
2. (a) Rs 2,190   (b) Rs 2,528   (c) Rs 9,650
   (d) Rs 15,451   (e) Rs 72,050
3. (a) Rs 1,006   (b) Rs 3,955   (c) Rs 9,629
   (d) Rs 16,776   (e) Rs 3,650
4. (a) Profit; Rs 15   (b) Loss; Rs 750   (c) Rs 58
   (d) Rs 2,110   (e) Profit; Rs 780   (f) Rs 528; Rs 44

Exercise 2.3

1. (a) 2,51,412   (b) 2,83,156   (c) 3,28,510
   (d) 1,58,219   (e) 4,48,592   (f) 36,27,744
   (g) 22,01,384   (h) 35,71,875   (i) 3,26,027
   (j) 36,13,732   (k) 20,29,060   (l) 5,44,84,540

Exercise 2.4

1. (a) Q – 248; R – 38   (b) Q – 733; R – 28
   (c) Q – 969; R – 2   (d) Q – 397; R – 45
   (e) Q – 693; R – 7   (f) Q – 815; R – 6
   (g) Q – 839; R – 10   (h) Q – 696; R – 30
   (i) Q – 809; R – 21   (j) Q – 1316; R – 4
   (k) Q – 1201; R – 20   (l) Q – 562; R – 17

Exercise 2.5

1. (a) 5,135 copies   (b) 8784 km
   (c) 4,617 kilometres   (d) Rs 4,38,465
   (e) Rs 3000   (f) 981 boxes
   (g) 1,080 toys

Exercise 2.6

1. (a) Which is costlier and by how much?
   (b) How much did he get in all?
   (c) What was the cost for each student?
   (d) How many packets did the factory need?

Chapter Check-up

1. (a) 49,581   (b) 3,99,908
   (c) 8,999   (d) 23,375
   (e) 16,743   (f) 55,038
2. (a) 3,12,915   (b) 2,09,430
   (c) 13,87,826   (d) 2,95,809
3. (a) Q – 238; R – 2   (b) Q – 409; R – 5
   (c) Q – 2206; R – 8   (d) Q – 1260; R – 40
4. (a) 63,840 onions
   (b) 73 boxes
   (c) 25,674 books
   (d) Selling price of refrigerator – Rs 12,450; Selling price of television set – Rs 12,050
6. (a) 9,110   (b) 71,880
   (c) 178   (d) 952

Chapter 3 – Factors and Multiples

Exercise 3.2

1. (a) 1×3×17   (b) 2×2×3×5   (c) 2×3×3×5
   (d) 2×2×2×2×2   (e) 2×2×2×3   (f) 3×3×7
   (g) 3×3×3×3   (h) 2×2×2×3×3   (i) 2×2×7
   (j) 2×2×2×11   (k) 2×31   (l) 3×3×5

(m) 2×23   (n) 2×2×11   (o) 5×13
(p) 2×5×7   (q) 3×29   (r) 2×47

Exercise 3.3

2. (a) 2   (b) 8   (c) 5   (d) 16
   (e) 4   (f) 9   (g) 9   (h) 1
   (i) 3   (j) 3   (k) 2   (l) 4
   (m) 1   (n) 3   (o) 5   (p) 2

Challenge – Page 52

12th October

Exercise 3.4

2. (a) 288   (b) 39   (c) 2730   (d) 60
   (e) 1368   (f) 168   (g) 450   (h) 567
   (i) 126   (j) 672   (k) 288   (l) 5184
   (m) 90   (n) 60   (o) 96   (p) 60
   (q) 90   (r) 252   (s) 180   (t) 378

Chapter Check-up

3. (a) $2 \times 2 \times 2 \times 2 \times 3$ (b) 3×13
   (c) $2 \times 2 \times 3 \times 5$ (d) 3×29
   (e) $2 \times 2 \times 23$
4. (a) 8   (b) 14   (c) 4   (d) 14
   (e) 1   (f) 6   (g) 14   (h) 8
5. (a) 252   (b) 600   (c) 78   (d) 266
   (e) 42   (f) 224   (g) 264   (h) 15,912

Chapter 4 – Fractions

Exercise 4.1

1. (a) $\frac{2}{4}$ (b) $\frac{4}{6}$
   (c) $\frac{2}{10}$ (d) $\frac{4}{10}$
   (e) $\frac{2}{6}$ (f) $\frac{4}{14}$

2. (a) $\frac{3}{12}$ (b) $\frac{9}{15}$
   (c) $\frac{3}{18}$ (d) $\frac{3}{15}$
   (e) $\frac{6}{15}$ (f) $\frac{12}{15}$

3. (b) $\frac{1}{4} = \frac{2}{8} = \frac{3}{12} = \frac{4}{16}$
   (c) $\frac{2}{3} = \frac{4}{6} = \frac{6}{9} = \frac{8}{12}$
   (d) $\frac{2}{5} = \frac{4}{10} = \frac{6}{15} = \frac{8}{20}$
   (e) $\frac{3}{4} = \frac{6}{8} = \frac{9}{12} = \frac{12}{16}$

4. (a) $\frac{1}{3} = \frac{2}{6} = \frac{3}{9} = \frac{4}{12}$
   (b) $\frac{5}{6} = \frac{10}{12} = \frac{15}{18} = \frac{20}{24}$

5. (a) E   (b) NE   (c) NE
   (d) NE   (e) E   (f) E

6. (a) $\frac{1}{4}$ (b) $\frac{2}{7}$ (c) $\frac{7}{8}$
   (d) $\frac{1}{3}$ (e) $\frac{1}{2}$ (f) $\frac{11}{15}$

Exercise 4.2

1. (a) $\frac{2}{3}$ (b) $\frac{3}{4}$ (c) $\frac{2}{3}$
   (d) $\frac{3}{4}$ (e) $\frac{2}{3}$ (f) $\frac{3}{5}$

2. (a) $\frac{1}{3}$ (b) $\frac{1}{2}$ (c) $\frac{3}{4}$
   (d) $\frac{2}{3}$ (e) $\frac{4}{5}$ (f) $\frac{2}{3}$
   (g) $\frac{4}{5}$ (h) $\frac{1}{5}$

3. (c), (d), (e), and (f)

Exercise 4.3

1. (a) >   (b) >   (c) <
   (d) >   (e) <   (f) <
   (g) >   (h) <
2. (a) >   (b) >   (c) >
   (d) <   (e) <   (f) >
   (g) <   (h) >

3. (a) $\frac{9}{21} < \frac{9}{19} < \frac{9}{16} < \frac{9}{15} < \frac{9}{10}$
   (b) $\frac{1}{15} < \frac{3}{15} < \frac{6}{15} < \frac{12}{15} < \frac{14}{15}$
   (c) $\frac{1}{6} < \frac{2}{3} < \frac{3}{4} < \frac{7}{8}$
   (d) $\frac{3}{12} < \frac{2}{6} < \frac{2}{4} < \frac{7}{8}$
   (e) $\frac{1}{3} < \frac{1}{2} < \frac{2}{3} < \frac{3}{4}$
   (f) $\frac{1}{2} < \frac{6}{10} < \frac{2}{3} < \frac{4}{5} < \frac{5}{6}$

4. (a) $\frac{10}{14} > \frac{10}{15} > \frac{10}{20} > \frac{10}{22} > \frac{10}{35}$
   (b) $\frac{15}{19} > \frac{11}{19} > \frac{10}{19} > \frac{9}{19} > \frac{8}{19}$
   (c) $\frac{5}{6} > \frac{2}{3} > \frac{1}{2} > \frac{1}{5}$
   (d) $\frac{3}{4} > \frac{5}{12} > \frac{2}{6} > \frac{1}{8}$
   (e) $\frac{5}{6} > \frac{3}{4} > \frac{2}{3} > \frac{3}{5}$
   (f) $\frac{11}{12} > \frac{7}{9} > \frac{3}{4} > \frac{2}{3} > \frac{5}{8}$

Challenge – Page 66

Red $\frac{1}{8}$ Blue $\frac{1}{16}$ Green $\frac{1}{16}$

Orange $\frac{1}{8}$ Squares $\frac{1}{8}$ Black $\frac{1}{16}$

Exercise 4.4

1. (a) $\frac{8}{9}$ (b) $1\frac{1}{28}$ (c) $\frac{33}{35}$ (d) $1\frac{3}{6}$

   (e) $1\frac{11}{20}$ (f) $1\frac{11}{42}$ (g) $\frac{11}{16}$ (h) $\frac{5}{8}$

   (i) $1\frac{1}{4}$ (j) $\frac{15}{16}$ (k) $\frac{37}{56}$ (l) $3\frac{4}{7}$

   (m) $3\frac{4}{35}$ (n) $4\frac{8}{91}$ (o) $5\frac{8}{35}$ (p) $3\frac{3}{4}$

   (q) $5\frac{5}{12}$ (r) $3\frac{5}{3}$ (s) $7\frac{1}{4}$ (t) $\frac{13}{2}$

Exercise 4.5

1. (a) $\frac{1}{4}$ (b) $\frac{5}{12}$ (c) $\frac{1}{12}$ (d) $\frac{1}{2}$

   (e) $\frac{1}{6}$ (f) $\frac{4}{9}$ (g) $\frac{1}{5}$ (h) $\frac{5}{8}$

   (i) $\frac{9}{10}$ (j) $1\frac{27}{35}$ (k) $2\frac{2}{3}$ (l) $4\frac{1}{4}$

   (m) $2\frac{2}{3}$ (n) $7\frac{1}{3}$ (o) $4\frac{1}{12}$ (p) $10\frac{97}{112}$

Problem Solving – Page 71

(a) Add; $\frac{3}{4}$ allowance

(b) Add; $\frac{5}{8}$ homework

(c) Subtract; $2\frac{3}{8}$ litres

(d) Subtract; $1\frac{5}{6}$ ribbon

(e) Subtract; $\frac{1}{15}$ cup

(f) Add; $1\frac{3}{8}$ km

(g) Add; $\frac{23}{56}$ collection

(h) Subtract; $\frac{5}{12}$ hour

Exercise 4.6

1. (a) $\frac{7}{2}$ (b) $\frac{32}{5}$ (c) 4 (d) $\frac{10}{3}$ (e) 1

   (f) 0 (g) 12 (h) 24 (i) $\frac{25}{12}$ (j) $\frac{8}{17}$

   (k) $\frac{15}{2}$ (l) $\frac{1}{2}$ (m) 0 (n) $\frac{3}{5}$ (o) 8

2. (a) $\frac{3}{8}$ (b) $\frac{8}{15}$ (c) $\frac{3}{8}$ (d) $\frac{35}{12}$ (e) $\frac{16}{15}$

   (f) $\frac{4}{35}$ (g) $\frac{1}{4}$ (h) $\frac{2}{15}$ (i) $\frac{7}{24}$ (j) $\frac{3}{8}$

   (k) $\frac{5}{66}$ (l) $\frac{1}{3}$ (m) $\frac{5}{7}$ (n) $\frac{1}{3}$ (o) 1

   (p) $\frac{3}{7}$

Exercise 4.7

1. (a) $\frac{6}{7}$ (b) $\frac{5}{6}$ (c) $\frac{8}{15}$ (d) 0 (e) $\frac{5}{8}$

   (f) $\frac{18}{7}$ (g) 1 (h) 3 (i) $\frac{16}{21}$ (j) $\frac{15}{16}$

   (k) 0 (l) 4 (m) $\frac{16}{5}$ (n) $\frac{7}{6}$ (o) $\frac{3}{4}$

   (p) 1 (q) $\frac{8}{7}$ (r) $\frac{3}{7}$ (s) $\frac{6}{5}$ (t) $\frac{8}{3}$

2. (a) 15 (b) 21 (c) 48 (d) 10 (e) 8

   (f) $\frac{3}{7}$ (g) $\frac{1}{5}$ (h) $\frac{1}{14}$ (i) $\frac{1}{36}$ (j) $\frac{1}{60}$

   (k) 3 (l) $\frac{25}{2}$ (m) $\frac{6}{35}$ (n) $\frac{3}{64}$ (o) 9

   (p) $\frac{98}{3}$ (q) $\frac{4}{55}$ (r) $\frac{3}{154}$ (s) $\frac{2}{25}$ (t) $\frac{120}{7}$

3. (a) $4\frac{1}{5}$ cans (b) 3 sheets (c) $\frac{2}{9}$

   (d) $\frac{1}{20}$ (e) 12 bowls (f) 4 people

Chapter Check-up

1. (a) $\frac{4}{5} = \frac{8}{10} = \frac{12}{15}$

   (b) $\frac{7}{9} = \frac{14}{18} = \frac{21}{27}$

   (c) $\frac{6}{11} = \frac{12}{22} = \frac{18}{33}$

2. (a) $\frac{2}{3}$ (b) $\frac{2}{3}$ (c) $\frac{9}{10}$

3. (a) $\frac{1}{7} < \frac{1}{3}$ (b) $\frac{2}{9} < \frac{5}{9}$ (c) $\frac{3}{5} > \frac{2}{7}$ (d) $\frac{6}{9} > \frac{2}{5}$

4. (a) $\frac{10}{13}$ (b) $1\frac{1}{2}$ (c) $\frac{13}{9}$ or $1\frac{4}{9}$ (d) $\frac{31}{35}$

   (e) $2\frac{16}{45}$ (f) $\frac{3}{17}$ (g) $\frac{7}{36}$ (h) $1\frac{3}{10}$

5. (a) $\frac{10}{7}$ or $1\frac{3}{7}$ (b) $\frac{28}{33}$ (c) 0

   (d) $\frac{1}{6}$ (e) $\frac{5}{33}$ (f) $\frac{8}{21}$

   (g) $\frac{4}{35}$ (h) $\frac{8}{5}$ or $1\frac{3}{5}$ (i) $\frac{64}{3}$

   (j) $\frac{35}{33}$

6. (a) 50 candles (b) $\frac{17}{4}$ or $4\frac{1}{4}$ hours (c) $1\frac{7}{12}$ hours

Chapter 5 – Decimals

Exercise 5.2

2. (a) 8 (b) 4 (c) 1 (d) 5 (e) 6 (f) 2
3. (a) 4.7 (b) 58.96 (c) 5.783
4. (a) 1.5, 1.6, 1.7 (b) 5.95, 5.96, 5.97
   (c) 12.1, 12.2, 12.3 (d) 8.004, 8.005, 8.006
   (e) 6.05, 6.06, 6.07 (f) 4.26, 4.27, 4.28

Exercise 5.3

1. (a) 6.79 (b) 5.108 (c) 3.085
   (d) 0.867 (e) 31.28 (f) 17.521
2. (a) 9.683 (b) 1.106 (c) 43.075
   (d) 56.008 (e) 0.387 (f) 20.009

3. (a) Decimal – $9 + 0.8 + 0.07 + 0.005$
   Fraction – $9 + \frac{8}{10} + \frac{7}{100} + \frac{5}{1000}$

   (b) Decimal – $20 + 3 + 0.07 + 0.006$
   Fraction – $20 + 3 + \frac{7}{100} + \frac{6}{1000}$

(c) Decimal – 10 + 4 + 0.8 + 0.007

Fraction – $10 + 4 + \frac{8}{10} + \frac{7}{1000}$

(d) Decimal – 300 + 90 + 6 + 0.9 + 0.09

Fraction – $300 + 90 + 6 + \frac{9}{10} + \frac{9}{100}$

(e) Decimal – 80 + 7 + 0.1

Fraction – $80 + 7 + \frac{1}{10}$

4. (a) 0.72   (b) 0.8   (c) 0.09   (d) 1.37
   (e) 0.186   (f) 0.004   (g) 1.171   (h) 45.4
   (i) 0.42   (j) 18.76   (k) 0.23   (l) 901.8

5. (a) $\frac{4}{100}$ (b) $\frac{1563}{100}$ (c) $\frac{249}{10}$ (d) $\frac{175}{1000}$

   (e) $\frac{26004}{1000}$ (f) $\frac{86}{100}$ (g) $\frac{131}{100}$ (h) $\frac{7105}{1000}$

Challenge – Page 89
0.872   0.278   7.82

Exercise 5.6
1. (a) 26.91   (b) 16.09   (c) 10.8
   (d) 612.2   (e) 12.5   (f) 178.31
   (g) 10.46   (h) 41.94   (i) 35.11

Exercise 5.7
1. (a) 5.16   (b) 9.17   (c) 2.68   (d) 6.27
   (e) 0.9   (f) 5.71   (g) 0.39   (h) 1.96
   (i) 4.85   (j) 3.72   (k) 8.35   (l) 3.05
2. 7.9
3. 11.04
5. (a) 1.25 seconds (b) 0.53 seconds

Problem Solving – Page 93
1. 6.5 points   2. 78.5 km
3. 9.25 m   4. 5.83 cm
5. Shamin; 15.5   6. Team B; 85 points
7. Swapneel   8. 37.5 km

Exercise 5.8
1. (a) 22.5   (b) 19.89   (c) 0.32
   (d) 22.86   (e) 26.4   (f) 8.08
2. (a) 1016; 101.6; 10.16
   (b) 1560; 156; 15.6
3. (a) 47.7   (b) 92.4   (c) 21.6
   (d) 129.2   (e) 6.9   (f) 58.73
   (g) 139.36   (h) 9.84

Exercise 5.9
2. (a) 9.13   (b) 0.13   (c) 45.37   (d) 56.2
   (e) 5.91   (f) 0.36   (g) 3.06   (h) 0.4
3. (a) 15.05   (b) 2.15   (c) 0.775   (d) 4.575
   (e) 1.85   (f) 0.65   (g) 0.534   (h) 9.045

Exercise 5.10
1. (a) 282.5   (b) 8.1   (c) 12.3   (d) 11
   (e) 1,673   (f) 319   (g) 14   (h) 80
2. (a) 0.576   (b) 0.83   (c) 0.09   (d) 3.6
   (e) 0.531   (f) 0.62   (g) 0.028   (h) 0.04
3. (a) 10 (b) 10 (c) 100 (d) 10 (e) 100 (f) 100
4. (a) 10 (b) 10 (c) 10 (d) 10 (e) 100 (f) 100

Exercise 5.11
1. Rs 27.50;   Rs 92;   Rs 8.50;   Rs 12;   Rs 122

2.

Item	Quantity	Price (Rs)
Toothpaste	2	57.00
Rice	5 kg	126.25
Wheat flour	5 kg	92.50
Biscuits	3 packets	35.25
	Total	311.00

Item	Quantity	Price (Rs)
Soap	2	30.00
Rice	10 kg	252.50
Washing powder	1 kg	43.00
Biscuits	5 packets	58.75
Buns	6 pieces	25.20
	Total	409.45

Exercise 5.12
1. 3 adult tickets; 1 child ticket
2. 8 large packets; 7 small packets of popcorn
3. 4 toy cars; 2 toy trucks
4. 8 red trays; 8 blue trays
5. 5 coupons of Rs 7.50 each; 3 coupons of Rs 10 each

Chapter Check-up
4. (a) 8.87   (b) 28.95   (c) 11.85   (d) 1.9
   (e) 0.08   (f) 1.85   (g) 2.93   (h) 8,570
   (i) 9.61   (j) 92   (k) 0.29
5. Rs 75
6. Rs 7.50
7. Rs 552.50
8. Rs 25.50
9. 12 m
10. 24.15 points
11. 1.8 cm

Chapter 6 – Geometry Basics
Exercise 6.1
4. (a) Obtuse angle   (b) Right angle
   (c) Acute angle   (d) Obtuse angle
   (e) Acute angle   (f) Straight angle
   (g) Right angle   (h) Acute angle

Challenge – Page 114
1. $\angle$ AOE   2. $\angle$ AOD   3. $\angle$ AOC   4. $\angle$ AOB
5. $\angle$ BOE   6. $\angle$ BOD   7. $\angle$ BOC   8. $\angle$ COE
9. $\angle$ COD   10. $\angle$ DOE

Chapter Check-up
1. (a) one   (b) line   (c) line segment
   (d) Right angle   (e) rays   (f) 90°; 180°
   (g) Acute angle

Chapter 7 – Exploring Shapes and Patterns

Exercise 7.2
1. (a), (d)
2. (b), (c)
4. H, I, N, O, S, X, Z
5. 11, 88, 808, 818, 1001, 1881
6. Largest – 8888; Smallest – 1001

Exercise 7.3
1. (a) $\frac{1}{3}$ (b) $\frac{1}{3}$ (c) $\frac{1}{3}$ (d) $\frac{1}{3}$
   (e) $\frac{1}{6}$ (f) $\frac{1}{6}$ (g) $\frac{1}{6}$

Challenge – Page 132
Cards 3, 5, 6 will look different on a half turn. Since the second row shows that they are the same, none of them have been turned. Card 4 is the only card that looks the same on a half turn. Therefore, Card 4 is the card that has been rotated $\frac{1}{2}$ turn.

Chapter Check-up
1. (b); (c); (e)
2. (a) $\frac{1}{2}$ turn (b) $\frac{1}{2}$ turn (c) $\frac{1}{4}$ turn
   (d) $\frac{1}{2}$ turn (e) $\frac{1}{2}$ turn (f) $\frac{1}{4}$ turn
3. (a) $\frac{1}{6}$ turn (b) $\frac{1}{3}$ turn (c) $\frac{1}{3}$ turn
   (d) $\frac{1}{3}$ turn (e) $\frac{1}{6}$ turn (f) $\frac{1}{3}$ turn

Chapter 8 – Measurement

Exercise 8.2
1. (a) 12 cm   (b) 9.6 m
   (c) 100 m   (d) 380 cm
   (e) 87 cm   (f) 720 mm
   (g) 0.70 m   (h) 8 mm
   (i) 92 mm   (j) 4.2 cm
2. (a) 6200 m   (b) 120 m
   (c) 9100 m   (d) 6.3 km
   (e) 1.10 km   (f) 2.8 km
3. (b) 98 m 98 cm (c) 16.24 m
   (d) 11.2 cm   (e) 28 cm 7 mm
   (f) 498 mm

Problem Solving – Page 145
(a) 95 cm   (b) 500 hops   (c) 22.4 km
(d) 1.63 m   (e) 50 books   (f) 11 cm
(g) 21.4 cm

Fill in the blanks
(a) 1.5 mm   (b) 5.8 mm   (c) 9.8 mm   (d) 0.62 mm

Exercise 8.3
1. (a) 19 kg 386 g   (b) 0 kg 832 g
   (c) 2614 g   (d) 8610 g
   (e) 3 kg 246 g   (f) 11.296 kg
2. (a) 420 g   (b) 900 g   (c) 1600 g   (d) 5190 g

3. (a) 0.125 kg   (b) 0.9 kg   (c) 0.12 kg   (d) 9.5 kg
4. (a) 0.715 kg   (b) 60 g   (c) 2.375 kg
   (d) 1040 g   (e) 12100 g   (f) 8.008 kg
   (g) 0.932 kg   (h) 350 g   (i) 6.125 kg
5. (a) 20 eggs   (b) 33.75 kg (c) 2.50 kg

Exercise 8.4
2. 1300 mℓ; 15,500 mℓ; 350 mℓ; 900 mℓ
3. 0.335 ℓ; 0.95 ℓ; 2.5 ℓ; 5.25 ℓ
4. (a) 400 mℓ (b) 8030 mℓ (c) 140 mℓ
   (d) 0.75 ℓ (e) 15350 mℓ (f) 0.10 ℓ
   (g) 4 ℓ (h) 1.84 ℓ (i) 1250 mℓ
5. (a) Yes   (b) 6 cups   (c) 1.2 ℓ

Exercise 8.5
1. (a) 29 m 6 cm   (b) 8 cm 4 mm
   (c) 12 kg   (d) 3 kg 250 g
   (e) 3 ℓ 150 mℓ (f) 8 ℓ 100 mℓ
2. (a) 3 m 50 cm   (b) 5 cm 9 mm
   (c) 1 kg 100 g   (d) 3 kg 750 g
   (e) 1 ℓ 700 mℓ (f) 8 ℓ 500 mℓ
3. (a) 4 m 25 cm   (b) 9 m 65 cm
   (c) 350 mℓ (d) 3 kg 850 g
   (e) 27 kg 750 g

Exercise 8.6
1. (a) 9 g   (b) 100 g   (c) 500 g   (d) 120 g
   (e) 30 ℓ (f) 1 ℓ (g) 100 g   (h) 300 mℓ
   (i) 8 cm   (j) 50 cm   (k) 900 m   (l) 2 mm
2. (a) kg   (b) g   (c) m   (d) litres   (e) cm   (f) mℓ

Chapter Check-up
1. (a) 800 m   (b) 1.5 km   (c) 8,400 m
   (d) 18 cm   (e) 7.2 m   (f) 350 cm
   (g) 12 mm   (h) 22 cm   (i) 3 mm
2. (a) 0.85 kg   (b) 90 g   (c) 1.38 kg
   (d) 900 g   (e) 1150 g   (f) 2.2 kg
3. (a) 500 mℓ (b) 170 mℓ (c) 1.88 ℓ
   (d) 7250 mℓ (e) 0.2 ℓ (f) 0.95 ℓ
6. (a) 3 m 20 cm cloth   (b) 8 kg 350 g   (c) 3 ℓ 800 mℓ

Chapter 9 – Area and Perimeter

Exercise 9.1
1. (a) 240 cm   (b) 550 cm
   (c) 344 cm   (d) 160 cm
   (e) 320 cm   (f) 240 cm
2. (b) 20 cm   (c) 44 cm   (d) 72 cm
   (e) 100 cm   (f) 120 cm   (g) 164 cm
   (h) 220 cm   (i) 252 cm   (j) 368 cm
3. (b) 12 cm   (c) 14 cm   (d) 18 cm
   (e) 14 cm   (f) 18 cm   (g) 20 cm
   (h) 22cm   (i) 28 cm   (j) 32 cm
4. (b) 10 cm   (c) 16 cm   (d) 24 cm
   (e) 30 cm   (f) 43 cm   (g) 58 cm
   (d) 75 cm   (i) 96 cm   (j) 139 cm

Exercise 9.2
5. (a) 45 sq. cm   (b) 120 sq. cm   (c) 65 sq. cm
   (d) 22.5 sq. cm (e) 18.9 sq. cm (f) 52 sq. cm

5. (b) 12 cm   (c) 8 cm   (d) 4 cm
    (e) 6 cm   (f) 28 cm   (g) 10 cm
    (h) 17 cm   (i) 11 cm   (j) 17 cm

Exercise 9.5

5. (a) 54 m   (b) 156 m; Rs 15,288
    (c) 1,400 m or 1.4 km   (d) 25 cm
    (e) 8,100 sq. m   (f) 50 cm
    (g) 1500 tiles

Chapter Check-up

2. (a) Perimeter – 28 cm; Area – 49 sq. cm
    (b) Perimeter – 32 m; Area – 55 sq. m
4. (a) sq. cm   (b) sq. cm   (c) sq. m
    (d) sq. km   (e) sq. km   (f) sq. cm
6. (a) 1,290 m or 1.29 km
    (b) 16 m
    (c) Area – 70 sq. m; Perimeter – 34 m
    (d) 2 cm

Chapter 10 – Volume and Nets

Exercise 10.2

2. (a) 60 cu. cm   (b) 60 cu. cm   (c) 384 cu. mm
3. (a) 120 cu. cm   (b) 100 cu. cm   (c) 288 cu. cm
    (d) 120 cu. cm   (e) 10 cu. cm   (f) 90 cu. cm
4. (a) 3,120 cu. mm
    (b) 1,485 cu. cm
    (c) 384 cu. m
5. (a) 168 cu. m   (b) 5 cm   (c) 4 cm
    (d) 11 mm   (e) 108 cu. m
6. (a) 1,344 cu. cm   (b)13,500 cu. cm
    (c) 5,400 cu. cm   (d) 60,000 cu. cm

Challenge – Page 176

4 cu. cm

Challenge – Page 179

21 (7 × 3)

Chapter Check-up

6. (a) 90 cu. m   (b) 512 cu. cm
    (c) 10 cm   (d) 600 cu. cm

Chapter 11 – Time and Temperature

Exercise 11.1

1. (a) 480 minutes   (b) 660 minutes
    (c) 420 minutes   (d) 560 minutes
    (e) 192 minutes   (f) 282 minutes
2. (a) 12 hours   (b) 2 hours 12 minutes
    (c) 2 hours 10 minutes   (d) 6 hours
    (e) 6 hours 50 minutes   (f) 8 hours 20 minutes
3. (a) 780 seconds   (b) 300 seconds
    (c) 1,560 seconds   (d) 630 seconds
    (e) 900 seconds   (f) 2,700 seconds
4. (a) 14 minutes   (b) 8 minutes
    (c) 4 minutes 40 seconds   (d) 10 minutes
    (e) 1 minute 33 seconds   (f) 15 minutes 50 seconds
5. (a) 660 seconds

(b) 8 minutes 24 seconds
(c) 5 minutes
(d) 300 caps
(e) She jogged for the same time on both days

Exercise 11.2

1. (a) 11 minutes   (b) 5 minutes 5 seconds
    (c) 3 hours 10 minutes   (d) 3 hours 20 minutes
    (e) 8 years   (f) 23 years
2. (a) 1 min 8 seconds   (b) 7 min 25 seconds
    (c) 5 hours 40 minutes   (d) 4 hours 50 minutes
    (e) 3 years   (f) 1 year 10 months
3. (a) 1 hour 20 minutes   (b) 17 years 3 months
    (c) 6 hours
    (e) 1 hour 25 minutes   (d) 42 seconds

Challenge – Page 193

10 : 20

Exercise 11.3

1. (a) 5:45 p.m.   (b) 2:00 p.m.   (c) 3:15 p.m.
    (d) 12:45 p.m.   (e) 12 midnight   (f) 2:45 p.m.
2. (a) 15th January   (b) 13th December   (c) 18th April
    (d) 21st March   (e) 14th December   (f) 16th May
3. (a) 19th February
    (b) 3:25 p.m.
    (c) 8th September
    (d) 21st August
    (e) 2:35 p.m.

Exercise 11.4

1. (b) 42°C   (c) 45°C
    (d) 5°C   (e) 0°C
    (f) 38.5°C
3. (a) 20 minutes   (b) 82°C

Chapter Check-up

1. (a) 200 min   (b) 9 h 20 min
    (c) 690 seconds   (d) 16 min 20 sec
    (e) 11 min 40 sec   (f) 1 year 11 months
    (g) 6 h 10 min
2. (a) 3:05 p.m.   (b) 2.30 p.m.
3. (a) 10th September   (b) 22nd October
5. (a) 2 h 30 min   (b) 30 minutes

Chapter 13 – Handling Data

Exercise 13.1

1. 6 hours   –   School
    9 hours   –   Sleep
    1 hour   –   Homework
    2 hour   –   Play
    5 hours   –   Others
    1 hour   –   TV
3. (a)   (i)   Ada   –   10 votes
          (ii)   Rashi   –   10 votes
          (iii)   Mira   –   5 votes
          (iv)   Anita   –   15 votes

Challenge – Page 216

22nd January; 12th March

Chapter Check-up

1. (a) Maths   – $\frac{1}{2}$ (b) 6 hours

    Science   – $\frac{1}{4}$ (c) 3 hours

    English   – $\frac{1}{8}$ (d) $1\frac{1}{2}$ hours

    Soc. Study – $\frac{1}{8}$

2. (a) Chips
  (b) Cake
  (c) Sandwich and *Samosa*
  (d) 19 children
  (e) 63 children

3. (a) December and January
  (b) October
  (c) 400 sweaters
  (d) 200 sweaters